Taste of Home

Dessert Lovers

COOKBOOK

Taste of Home

Dessert Lovers

COOKBOOK

Reader's Digest

The Reader's Digest Association, Inc.

Pleasantville, NY/Montreal

Pictured on Front Cover: Chocolate Cookie Torte, page 33.

Pictured on Back Cover: Very Chocolate Brownies, page 10; Mint Chip Ice Cream, page 104; Deluxe Chip Cheesecake, page 46.

Pictured on page 2: Chocolate Malted Cookies, page 24

Pictured on page 6: Rocky Road Freeze, page 113

For more Reader's Digest products and information, visit our website at www.rd.com

Printed in China

Editor: Jean Steiner

Art Director: Catherine Fletcher

Executive Editor: Heidi Reuter Lloyd

Associate Editor: Beth Wittlinger

Food Editor: Janaan Cunningham

Associate Food Editors: Coleen Martin, Diane Werner

Senior Recipe Editor: Sue A. Jurack

Recipe Editor: Janet Briggs

Food Photography: Rob Hagen, Dan Roberts

Senior Food Photography Artist: Stephanie Marchese

Food Photography Artist: Julie Ferron

Photo Studio Manager: Anne Schimmel

Senior Vice President, Editor in Chief: Catherine Cassidy

President: Barbara Newton

Chairman and Founder: Roy Reiman

Heavenly Cookbook Serves Up Divine Desserts!

Family and Friends will be on cloud nine when *Taste of Home* DESSERT LOVERS COOKBOOK becomes part of your cookbook collection. Why? Because the most luscious, delicious desserts will be gracing your dinner table throughout the year!

This fantastic book is filled with more than 240 sweet treats, including scrumptious bars and brownies, cookies, pretty cakes, tortes and cheese-cakes, pleasing pies, cobblers and puddings, elegant-looking cream puffs, trifles and eclairs, and refreshing refrigerator and freezer treats.

Fellow dessert lovers from across North America shared these divine recipes, which have appeared in past issues of *Taste of Home* magazine and its "sister" publications. Our home economists eagerly prepared and taste-tested them as well, compiling the best ones into this heavenly recipe collection.

If just looking at the decadent treats pictured in this *Taste of Home* DESSERT LOVERS COOKBOOK makes your mouth water, wait until you indulge in them!

Table of Contents

Bars &
Brownies

Very Chocolate Brownies, p. 10

Raspberry Almond Bars

(Pictured below)

A co-worker's mother gave me this gem of a recipe a few years back. I can never decide what's more appealing—the attractive look of the bars or their incredible aroma while they're baking! Everyone who tries these asks for the recipe.
—Mimi Priesman, Pace, Florida

1/2 cup butter
1 package (10 to 12 ounces) vanilla *or* white chips, *divided*
2 eggs
1/2 cup sugar
1 teaspoon almond extract
1 cup all-purpose flour
1/2 teaspoon salt
1/2 cup seedless raspberry jam
1/4 cup sliced almonds

In a saucepan, melt butter. Remove from the heat; add 1 cup chips (do not stir). In a small mixing bowl, beat eggs until foamy; gradually add sugar. Stir in chip mixture and almond extract. Combine flour and salt; add to egg mixture just until combined.

Spread half of the batter into a greased 9-in. square baking pan. Bake at 325° for 15-20 minutes or until golden brown.

In a small saucepan over low heat, melt jam; spread over warm crust. Stir remaining chips into the remaining batter; drop by teaspoonfuls over the jam layer. Sprinkle with almonds. Bake 30-35 minutes longer or until a toothpick inserted near the center comes out clean. Cool on a wire rack. Cut into bars. **Yield:** 2 dozen.

Very Chocolate Brownies

(Pictured on page 9)

I've spent years trying different recipes in search of the perfect brownie...and this scrumptious version might be it. The fluffy melt-in-your-mouth top layer is heavenly. —Arlene Butler, Ogden, Utah

4 squares (1 ounce *each*) unsweetened chocolate
3/4 cup butter
2 cups sugar
3 eggs
1 teaspoon vanilla extract
1 cup all-purpose flour
1 cup coarsely chopped walnuts
TOPPING:
1 cup (6 ounces) semisweet chocolate chips
1/4 cup water
2 tablespoons butter
1 cup heavy whipping cream, whipped

In a microwave or double boiler, melt chocolate and butter; cool for 10 minutes. Add sugar; mix well. Stir in eggs and vanilla. Add flour; mix well. Stir in the walnuts.

Line a 13-in. x 9-in. x 2-in. baking pan with foil and grease the foil. Pour batter into pan. Bake at 350° for 25-30 minutes or until a toothpick inserted near the center comes out with moist crumbs (do not overbake). Cool completely.

For topping, melt chocolate chips, water and butter in a microwave or double boiler; stir until smooth. Cool to room temperature. Fold in whipped cream. Spread over brownies. Chill before cutting. Store leftovers in the refrigerator. **Yield:** 3 dozen.

Cranberry Nut Bars

Each fall when cranberries are harvested, I buy many bags and put them in the freezer. That way I can enjoy these delicious berries all year long. This dessert featuring those ruby gems is a favorite at potluck suppers. —Ruth MacDougald
Wrentham, Massachusetts

2 eggs
1 cup sugar
1/2 teaspoon almond extract
1/2 teaspoon vanilla extract
1/8 teaspoon salt
1/2 cup butter, melted
1-1/2 cups all-purpose flour
1 teaspoon baking powder
2 cups fresh *or* frozen cranberries
1/2 cup chopped walnuts

In a mixing bowl, beat eggs, sugar, extracts and salt. Add butter. Combine flour and baking powder; gradually add to the sugar mixture and mix well. Fold in cranberries and nuts. Transfer to a greased 13-in. x 9-in. x 2-in. baking pan. Bake at 350° for 30-35 minutes or until golden brown. Cool on a wire rack. Cut into bars. **Yield:** 2 dozen.

Peppermint Patty Brownies

(Pictured above)

I add a special ingredient to these sweet and fudgy brownies—a layer of mint patties provides the rich, refreshing surprise. —Clara Bakke
Coon Rapids, Minnesota

1-1/2 cups butter, softened
3 cups sugar
5 eggs
1 tablespoon vanilla extract
2 cups all-purpose flour
1 cup baking cocoa
1 teaspoon baking powder
1 teaspoon salt
1 package (13 ounces) chocolate-covered peppermint patties

In a mixing bowl, cream butter and sugar. Add eggs, one at a time, beating well after each addition. Beat in vanilla. Combine the dry ingredients; add to creamed mixture and mix well. Spread two-thirds of the batter in a greased 13-in. x 9-in. x 2-in. baking pan. Arrange peppermint patties over top. Carefully spread remaining batter over patties.

Bake at 350° for 35-40 minutes or until edges begin to pull away from sides of pan and a toothpick inserted near the center comes out clean (top will appear uneven). Cool completely before cutting. **Yield:** 2 to 2-1/2 dozen.

Helping Hand

Let the kids help with the brownies by unwrapping the peppermint patties.

Chocolate Cherry Bars

(Pictured above)

These tempting bars are simple to make with cherry pie filling, crunchy almonds and chocolate chips. I took them to a church supper and everyone wanted the recipe. Some people said the sweet treats reminded them of chocolate-covered cherries.
—Tina Dierking, Canaan, Maine

1-3/4 cups all-purpose flour
  1 cup sugar
  1/4 cup baking cocoa
  1 cup cold butter
  1 egg, lightly beaten
  1 teaspoon almond extract
  1 can (21 ounces) cherry pie filling
  2 cups (12 ounces) semisweet chocolate
    chips
  1 cup chopped almonds

In a bowl, combine the flour, sugar and cocoa. Cut in butter until crumbly. Add egg and almond extract until blended; set aside 1 cup for topping. Press remaining crumb mixture into a greased 13-in. x 9-in. x 2-in. baking pan. Carefully top with pie filling. Combine chocolate chips, almonds and reserved crumb mixture; sprinkle over pie filling.

Bake at 350° for 35-40 minutes or until a toothpick inserted near the center comes out clean. Cool; refrigerate for at least 2 hours before cutting. **Yield:** 3 dozen.

Caramel Brownies

My family can't possibly eat all of the sweets I whip up, so my co-workers are more than happy to sample them—particularly these rich chewy brownies that are full of gooey caramel, chocolate chips and crunchy walnuts. —Clara Bakke
Coon Rapids, Minnesota

  2 cups sugar
  3/4 cup baking cocoa
  1 cup vegetable oil
  4 eggs
  1/4 cup milk
1-1/2 cups all-purpose flour
  1 teaspoon salt
  1 teaspoon baking powder
  1 cup (6 ounces) semisweet chocolate
    chips
  1 cup chopped walnuts, *divided*
  1 package (14 ounces) caramels
  1 can (14 ounces) sweetened condensed
    milk

In a mixing bowl, combine the sugar, cocoa, oil, eggs and milk. Combine the flour, salt and baking powder; add to egg mixture and mix until combined. Fold in chocolate chips and 1/2 cup walnuts. Spoon two-thirds of the batter into a greased 13-in. x 9-in. x 2-in. baking pan. Bake at 350° for 12 minutes.

Meanwhile, in a saucepan, heat the caramels and condensed milk over low heat until caramels are melted. Pour over baked brownie layer. Sprinkle with remaining walnuts. Drop remaining batter by teaspoonfuls over caramel layer; carefully swirl brownie batter with a knife. Bake 35-40 minutes longer or until a toothpick inserted near the center comes out with moist crumbs. Cool on a wire rack. **Yield:** 2 dozen.

Editor's Note: This recipe was tested with Hershey caramels.

Pear Custard Bars

When I take this crowd-pleasing treat to a potluck, I come home with an empty pan every time. Cooking and baking come naturally for me—as a farm girl, I helped my mother feed my 10 siblings.
—Jeannette Nord
San Juan Capistrano, California

1/2 cup butter, softened
1/3 cup sugar
3/4 cup all-purpose flour
1/4 teaspoon vanilla extract
2/3 cup chopped macadamia nuts

FILLING/TOPPING:
- 1 package (8 ounces) cream cheese, softened
- 1/2 cup sugar
- 1 egg
- 1/2 teaspoon vanilla extract
- 1 can (15-1/4 ounces) pear halves, drained
- 1/2 teaspoon sugar
- 1/2 teaspoon ground cinnamon

In a mixing bowl, cream butter and sugar. Beat in the flour and vanilla until combined. Stir in the nuts. Press into a greased 8-in. square baking pan. Bake at 350° for 20 minutes or until lightly browned. Cool on a wire rack. Increase heat to 375°.

In a mixing bowl, beat cream cheese until smooth. Add sugar, egg and vanilla; mix until combined. Pour over crust. Cut pears into 1/8-in. slices; arrange in a single layer over filling. Combine sugar and cinnamon; sprinkle over pears.

Bake at 375° for 28-30 minutes (center will be soft set and will become firmer upon cooling). Cool on a wire rack for 45 minutes. Cover and refrigerate for at least 2 hours before cutting. Store in the refrigerator. **Yield:** 16 bars.

Raspberry Swirled Brownies

Chocolate and raspberries are an irresistible combination. When entertaining, I dress up these fruity brownies with a dollop of whipped cream, fresh berries and a sprig of mint. —Iola Egle
McCook, Nebraska

- 1/2 cup butter, softened
- 1 cup sugar
- 1 can (16 ounces) chocolate syrup
- 4 eggs
- 1-1/2 cups all-purpose flour
- 1 package (3 ounces) cream cheese, softened
- 2/3 cup raspberry preserves
- 1 cup unsweetened raspberries

Whipped cream, fresh raspberries and mint, optional

In a mixing bowl, cream butter and sugar. Add chocolate syrup and eggs; mix well. Add flour and mix well. Beat cream cheese and preserves until smooth; gently stir in raspberries. Fold into the batter.

Spread in a greased 15-in. x 10-in. x 1-in. baking pan. Bake at 350° for 30-35 minutes or until a toothpick inserted near the center comes out clean. Cool. Cut into 2-1/2-in. diamonds. Garnish with whipped cream, raspberries and mint if desired.
Yield: about 2-1/2 dozen.

Fruit Cocktail Bars

(Pictured below)

My mother passed this recipe on to me. The moist bars have a delightful fruity taste, perfect for potlucks in winter when fresh fruit is limited.
—Linda Tackman, Escanaba, Michigan

- 1-1/2 cups sugar
- 2 eggs
- 1 can (17 ounces) fruit cocktail, undrained
- 1 teaspoon vanilla extract
- 2-1/4 cups all-purpose flour
- 1-1/2 teaspoons baking soda
- 1 teaspoon salt
- 1-1/3 cups flaked coconut
- 1 cup chopped walnuts

GLAZE:
- 1/2 cup sugar
- 1/4 cup butter
- 2 tablespoons milk
- 1/4 teaspoon vanilla extract

In a mixing bowl, cream sugar and eggs. Add fruit cocktail and vanilla; mix well. Combine the flour, baking soda and salt; add to the creamed mixture and mix well. Pour into a greased 15-in. x 10-in. x 1-in. baking pan. Sprinkle with coconut and walnuts. Bake at 350° for 20-25 minutes or until a toothpick inserted near the center comes out clean. Cool for 10 minutes.

In a saucepan, bring sugar, butter and milk to a boil. Remove from the heat; add vanilla and mix well. Drizzle over top. Cool. Cut into bars. **Yield:** 2 to 2-1/2 dozen.

Two-Tone Fudge Brownies

(Pictured below)

These moist fudgy brownies have a scrumptious topping that tastes just like chocolate chip cookie dough! My husband and I and our young sons enjoy church fellowship at frequent potluck meals. Everyone loves these brownies...and they make enough to feed a crowd. —Rebecca Kays
Klamath Falls, Oregon

    1 cup (6 ounces) semisweet chocolate
        chips
    1/2 cup butter, softened
    1 cup sugar
    3 eggs
    1 teaspoon vanilla extract
1-1/4 cups all-purpose flour
    1/4 teaspoon baking soda
    3/4 cup chopped walnuts
COOKIE DOUGH LAYER:
    1/2 cup butter, softened
    1/2 cup packed brown sugar
    1/4 cup sugar
    3 tablespoons milk
    1 teaspoon vanilla extract
    1 cup all-purpose flour
    1 cup (6 ounces) semisweet chocolate
        chips

In a microwave-safe bowl, melt chocolate chips. Cool slightly. In a mixing bowl, cream butter and sugar. Add eggs and vanilla; mix well. Stir in melted chocolate. Combine flour and baking soda; add to batter. Stir in walnuts.

Spread into a greased 13-in. x 9-in. x 2-in. baking pan. Bake at 350° for 16-22 minutes or until a toothpick inserted near the center comes out clean. Cool on a wire rack.

In a mixing bowl, cream butter and sugars. Beat in milk and vanilla. Gradually add flour. Stir in chocolate chips. Drop by tablespoonfuls over cooled brownies; carefully spread over top. Cut into squares. Store in the refrigerator. **Yield:** 4 dozen.

Editor's Note: Cookie dough layer is not baked and does not contain eggs.

Ginger Bars

We always had dessert when we visited my grandparents' farm, and this was one of our favorites. During harvesttime, my brothers and sisters and I would take this or another treat out to the field for the workers. —Deborah Haake
Minnetonka, Minnesota

    1 cup shortening
    1 cup sugar
    2 eggs
    1 cup water
    1/2 cup molasses
2-1/2 cups all-purpose flour
    1 teaspoon baking soda
    1 teaspoon ground cinnamon
    1/2 teaspoon ground cloves
    1/2 teaspoon ground ginger
    1/2 teaspoon salt
Confectioners' sugar, optional

In a mixing bowl, cream shortening and sugar. Add eggs; beat well. Beat in water and molasses. Combine flour, baking soda, cinnamon, cloves, ginger and salt; add to molasses mixture and mix well.

Spread into a greased 15-in. x 10-in. x 1-in. baking pan. Bake at 350° for 20-22 minutes or until a toothpick inserted near the center comes out clean. Cool. Dust with confectioners' sugar if desired. **Yield:** 16-20 servings.

Moist Cake Brownies

These brownies have been in my recipe collection since I was 9 years old. I've added to and altered the recipe over the years, and now I think it

has the perfect amount of everything, including semisweet and milk chocolate chips and pecans. They are my husband's and son's favorite.

—Louise Stacey, Dane, Wisconsin

    2/3 cup butter
    3/4 cup baking cocoa
    1/4 cup vegetable oil
      2 cups sugar
      4 eggs
      2 teaspoons vanilla extract
  1-1/2 cups all-purpose flour
      1 teaspoon baking powder
      1 teaspoon salt
    2/3 cup semisweet chocolate chips
    1/2 cup milk chocolate chips
      1 cup coarsely chopped pecans
Confectioners' sugar
Pecan halves, toasted, optional

Melt butter in a large saucepan. Whisk in cocoa and oil until smooth. Cook and stir over low heat until cocoa is blended. Remove from the heat; stir in sugar. Add eggs, one at a time, stirring well after each addition. Stir in vanilla. Combine flour, baking powder and salt; add to cocoa mixture. Stir in chocolate chips and nuts.

Spread into a greased 13-in. x 9-in. x 2-in. baking pan. Bake at 350° for 25-30 minutes or until a toothpick inserted near the center comes out clean. Cool. Dust with confectioners' sugar. Garnish with pecan halves if desired. **Yield:** 2 dozen.

Spread batter into a greased 13-in. x 9-in. x 2-in. baking pan. Combine brown sugar, walnuts, cinnamon and vanilla; sprinkle over batter. Bake at 350° for 30-35 minutes or until golden brown. Cool. Cut into squares. **Yield:** 12-16 servings.

Apple Walnut Squares

I make "apple everything" in fall when the new crop is in, and I was happy to add this delicious recipe to my apple dishes. A lady at church shared it with me. Sometimes I'll top the squares with a cream cheese frosting, especially for company.

—Leona Pecoraro, Ravenden, Arkansas

    1/2 cup shortening
      1 cup sugar
      1 egg
  1-1/2 cups all-purpose flour
  1-1/2 teaspoons baking soda
    1/2 teaspoon salt
  2-1/2 cups finely chopped peeled tart apples
    1/2 cup packed brown sugar
      1 cup chopped walnuts
      1 teaspoon ground cinnamon
      1 teaspoon vanilla extract

In a mixing bowl, cream shortening and sugar; beat in egg. Combine flour, baking soda and salt; gradually add to the creamed mixture and mix well (dough will be stiff). Stir in apples.

Chewy Pecan Pie Bars

(Pictured above)

This is one of my husband's favorite recipes. I've been making it for many years at his request.

—Judy Taylor, Shreveport, Louisiana

    1/4 cup butter, melted
      2 cups packed brown sugar
    2/3 cup all-purpose flour
      4 eggs
      2 teaspoons vanilla extract
    1/4 teaspoon baking soda
    1/4 teaspoon salt
      2 cups chopped pecans
Confectioners' sugar

Pour butter into a 13-in. x 9-in. x 2-in. baking pan; set aside. In a mixing bowl, combine brown sugar, flour, eggs, vanilla, baking soda and salt; mix well. Stir in pecans. Spread over butter. Bake at 350° for 30-35 minutes. Remove from the oven; immediately dust with confectioners' sugar. Cool before cutting. **Yield:** about 2 dozen.

Frosted Banana Bars

I make these moist bars whenever I have ripe bananas on hand, then store them in the freezer to share later at a potluck. With creamy frosting and big banana flavor, this treat is a crowd-pleaser.
—Debbie Knight, Marion, Iowa

1/2 cup butter, softened
1-1/2 cups sugar
2 eggs
1 cup (8 ounces) sour cream
1 teaspoon vanilla extract
2 cups all-purpose flour
1 teaspoon baking soda
1/4 teaspoon salt
2 medium ripe bananas, mashed (about 1 cup)
FROSTING:
1 package (8 ounces) cream cheese, softened
1/2 cup butter, softened
2 teaspoons vanilla extract
3-3/4 to 4 cups confectioners' sugar

In a mixing bowl, cream butter and sugar. Add eggs, sour cream and vanilla. Combine flour, baking soda and salt; gradually add to the creamed mixture. Stir in bananas.

Spread into a greased 15-in. x 10-in. x 1-in. baking pan. Bake at 350° for 20-25 minutes or until a toothpick inserted near the center comes out clean. Cool.

For frosting, in a mixing bowl, beat cream cheese, butter and vanilla. Gradually beat in enough confectioners' sugar to achieve desired consistency. Frost bars. Store in the refrigerator. **Yield:** 3-4 dozen.

Lemon Graham Squares

My aunt Jackie brought these lemon bars to every family gathering. They're my favorite lemon dessert. The crispy top and bottom give a nice texture.
—Janis Plourde
Smooth Rock Falls, Ontario

1 can (14 ounces) sweetened condensed milk
1/2 cup lemon juice
1-1/2 cups graham cracker crumbs (about 24 squares)
3/4 cup all-purpose flour
1/3 cup packed brown sugar
1/2 teaspoon baking powder
Pinch salt
1/2 cup butter, melted

In a bowl, combine the milk and lemon juice; mix well and set aside. In another bowl, combine the cracker crumbs, flour, brown sugar, baking powder and salt. Stir in butter until crumbly.

Press half of the crumb mixture into a greased 9-in. square baking dish. Pour lemon mixture over crust; sprinkle with remaining crumbs. Bake at 375° for 20-25 minutes or until lightly browned. Cool on a wire rack. **Yield:** 3 dozen.

Dark Chocolate Mocha Brownies

Dark chocolate is a favorite around our house, so these frosted brownies are a hit. I came up with this treat by reworking a recipe I've used for a long time.
—Linda McCoy, Oostburg, Wisconsin

2 cups packed brown sugar
1 cup butter, melted
3 eggs
1 tablespoon instant coffee granules
2 teaspoons vanilla extract
1 cup all-purpose flour
1 cup baking cocoa
1/2 teaspoon baking powder
1/2 teaspoon salt
6 ounces bittersweet chocolate, coarsely chopped
FROSTING:
1/4 cup butter, melted
3 tablespoons sour cream
2 teaspoons vanilla extract
2-3/4 to 3 cups confectioners' sugar
2 ounces grated bittersweet chocolate

In a mixing bowl, combine brown sugar and butter. Beat in eggs, one at a time. Add coffee and vanilla; mix well. Combine the flour, cocoa, baking powder and salt; add to sugar mixture and mix well. Stir in chocolate.

Spread into a greased 13-in. x 9-in. x 2-in. baking pan. Bake at 350° for 25-30 minutes or until a toothpick inserted near the center comes out clean. Cool on a wire rack.

For frosting, combine butter, sour cream and vanilla. Gradually stir in sugar until frosting reaches desired consistency. Frost brownies. Sprinkle with grated chocolate. **Yield:** 5 dozen.

Coffee Clue

Use hazelnut- or vanilla-flavored instant coffee granules in the brownies for a subtle taste twist.

Chunky Blond Brownies

Every bite of these chewy brownies is packed with chunks of white and semisweet chocolate and macadamia nuts. We have lots of excellent cooks in this rural community, so it's a challenge coming up with a potluck offering that stands out. These usually do—and they're snapped up fast.
—Rosemary Dreiske, Keldron, South Dakota

1/2 cup butter, softened
3/4 cup sugar
3/4 cup packed brown sugar
2 eggs
2 teaspoons vanilla extract
1-1/2 cups all-purpose flour
1 teaspoon baking powder
1/2 teaspoon salt
1 cup vanilla or white chips
1 cup semisweet chocolate chunks
1 jar (3-1/2 ounces) macadamia nuts or 3/4 cup blanched almonds, chopped, divided

In a mixing bowl, cream the butter and sugars. Add the eggs and vanilla; mix well. Combine flour, baking powder and salt; add to creamed mixture and mix well. Stir in vanilla chips, chocolate chunks and 1/2 cup nuts.

Spoon into a greased 13-in. x 9-in. x 2-in. baking pan; spread to evenly cover bottom of pan. Sprinkle with remaining nuts. Bake at 350° for 25-30 minutes or until golden brown. Cool on a wire rack.
Yield: 2 dozen.

Brownie Pie à la Mode

Cutting brownies into wedges and topping them with fudge sauce dresses them up.
—Beverly Thornton, Cortlandt Manor, New York

1/2 cup sugar
2 tablespoons butter
2 tablespoons water
1-1/2 cups semisweet chocolate chips
2 eggs
1 teaspoon vanilla extract
2/3 cup all-purpose flour
1/4 teaspoon baking soda
1/4 teaspoon salt
3/4 cup chopped walnuts
FUDGE SAUCE:
1 cup (6 ounces) semisweet chocolate chips
1/2 cup evaporated milk
1/4 cup sugar
1 tablespoon butter
Vanilla ice cream

In a small saucepan over medium heat, bring sugar, butter and water to a boil. Remove from the heat; stir in chocolate chips until melted. In a mixing bowl, beat eggs and vanilla. Add chocolate mixture; mix well. Combine flour, baking soda and salt; add to chocolate mixture. Stir in walnuts. Pour into a greased 9-in. pie plate. Bake at 350° for 28-30 minutes or until a toothpick inserted near the center comes out clean. Cool on a wire rack.

For fudge sauce, heat chocolate chips, milk, sugar and butter in a microwave or double boiler until chocolate and butter are melted; stir until smooth. Drizzle some over pie. Cut into wedges; serve with ice cream and additional sauce. **Yield:** 6-8 servings.

Volcano Brownie Cups

I cherish recipes like this—without fuss or extra time, I can turn out an elegant, irresistible dessert that looks like I've been cooking all day. I enjoy entertaining, and these treats always elicit oohs and aahs from guests.
—Kellie Durazo, Merced, California

   1 cup butter, softened
1/2 cup sugar
   3 eggs
   3 egg yolks
   1 teaspoon vanilla extract
   2 cups (12 ounces) semisweet chocolate
      chips, melted
   1 cup all-purpose flour
1/4 teaspoon salt
   1 cup ground toasted pecans
   6 squares (1 ounce each) white baking
      chocolate
Confectioners' sugar

In a mixing bowl, cream butter and sugar. Add eggs, yolks and vanilla; mix well. Add melted chocolate. Combine flour and salt; add to creamed mixture. Stir in nuts. Spoon into six greased 10-oz. custard cups; place on a baking sheet. Bake at 350° for 10 minutes.

Push one square of chocolate into center of each brownie. Bake 18-20 minutes longer or until a toothpick inserted in the brownie comes out clean. Remove from the oven and let stand for 5 minutes. Run a knife around edge of custard cups; invert onto serving plates. Dust with confectioners' sugar. Serve warm. **Yield:** 6 servings.

   Editor's Note: To reheat, return brownie to custard cup and bake at 350° for 10 minutes.

Peanut Butter Swirl Brownies

Peanut butter and chocolate are always a delicious duo, but they're extra-special paired in this tempting treat. Even with a sizable collection of brownie recipes, I reach for this one quite often.
—Linda Craig, Hay River, Northwest Territories

1/2 cup butter, softened
2/3 cup sugar
1/2 cup packed brown sugar
   2 eggs
   2 tablespoons milk
3/4 cup all-purpose flour
1/2 teaspoon baking powder
1/4 teaspoon salt
1/4 cup creamy peanut butter
1/3 cup peanut butter chips
1/3 cup baking cocoa
1/2 cup semisweet chocolate chips

In a mixing bowl, cream butter and sugars. Add eggs and milk; mix well. Combine flour, baking powder and salt; add to creamed mixture and mix well.

   Divide batter in half. To one portion, add peanut butter and peanut butter chips; mix well. To the other portion, add the cocoa and chocolate chips; mix well.

   In a greased 9-in. square baking pan, spoon chocolate batter in eight mounds in a checkerboard pattern. Spoon seven mounds of peanut butter batter between the chocolate batter. Cut through batters with a knife to swirl. Bake at 350° for 25-30 minutes or until a toothpick inserted near the center comes out clean. Cool on a wire rack. **Yield:** 3 dozen.

Fudge-Topped Brownies

If you love brownies and fudge, why not combine the two? Mix up a pan of these exquisite brownies for any holiday or special gathering...or just when you want to treat yourself to the ultimate chocolate dessert.

—Judy Olson, Whitecourt, Alberta

1 cup butter
4 squares (1 ounce each) unsweetened chocolate
2 cups sugar
2 teaspoons vanilla extract
4 eggs
1-1/2 cups all-purpose flour
1 teaspoon baking powder
1/2 teaspoon salt
1 cup chopped walnuts

TOPPING:
4-1/2 cups sugar
1 can (12 ounces) evaporated milk
1/2 cup butter
1 package (12 ounces) semisweet chocolate chips
1 package (11-1/2 ounces) milk chocolate chips
1 jar (7 ounces) marshmallow creme
2 teaspoons vanilla extract
2 cups chopped walnuts

In a saucepan over low heat, melt butter and chocolate. Remove from heat. Blend in sugar and vanilla. Beat in eggs. Combine flour, baking powder and salt; add to chocolate mixture. Stir in nuts. Pour into a greased 13-in. x 9-in. x 2-in. baking pan. Bake at 350° for 25-30 minutes or until top springs back when lightly touched.

In a heavy saucepan, combine sugar, milk and butter; bring to a boil over medium heat. Reduce heat; simmer 5 minutes, stirring constantly. Remove from heat. Stir in chips, creme and vanilla; beat until smooth. Add nuts. Spread over warm brownies. Freeze until firm. Cut into 1-in. squares. Store in the refrigerator. **Yield:** about 10 dozen.

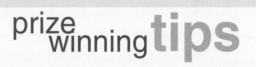

*To add a glossy look to your iced brownies, frost them while they are still warm.
—Juanita Thompson, Grand Rapids, Michigan

*I like to dress up my brownies for birthdays and other special occasions by garnishing them with whole strawberries and chocolate curls.
—Gertrude Sawatzky, MacGregor, Manitoba

*As a flavorful alternative, I will sometimes substitute mint extract for vanilla in my brownies.
—Andrea Hiebert, Dallas, Oregon

Brownie Kiss Cupcakes

It's fun to prepare individual brownie cupcakes with a chocolaty surprise inside. My goddaughter, Cara, asks me to make them for her birthday to share at school with her classmates. One year, she requested 32. I later found out she only needed 27 for her class...Wonder where the other five went!
—Pamela Lute, Mercersburg, Pennsylvania

1/3 cup butter, softened
1 cup sugar
2 eggs
1 teaspoon vanilla extract
3/4 cup all-purpose flour
1/2 cup baking cocoa
1/4 teaspoon baking powder
1/4 teaspoon salt
9 milk chocolate kisses

In a mixing bowl, cream the butter and sugar. Add eggs and vanilla; mix well. Combine the flour, cocoa, baking powder and salt; add to the creamed mixture and mix well.

Fill paper- or foil-lined muffin cups two-thirds full. Place a chocolate kiss, tip end down, in the center of each. Bake at 350° for 20-25 minutes or until the top of the brownie springs back when lightly touched. **Yield:** 9 cupcakes.

Cookies 'n' Cream Brownies

You won't want to frost these brownies, since the marbled top is too pretty to cover up. Besides, the tasty cream cheese layer makes them taste like they're already frosted. The crushed cookies add extra chocolate flavor and a fun crunch.
—Darlene Markel, Sublimity, Oregon

CREAM CHEESE LAYER:
1 package (8 ounces) cream cheese, softened
1/4 cup sugar
1 egg
1/2 teaspoon vanilla extract
BROWNIE LAYER:
1/2 cup butter, melted
1/2 cup sugar
1/2 cup packed brown sugar
1/2 cup baking cocoa
2 eggs
1/2 cup all-purpose flour
1 teaspoon baking powder
1 teaspoon vanilla extract
12 cream-filled chocolate sandwich cookies, crushed

In a small mixing bowl, beat the cream cheese, sugar, egg and vanilla until smooth; set aside. For brownie layer, combine butter, sugars and cocoa in a large mixing bowl; blend well. Add eggs, one at a time, beating well after each addition. Combine flour and baking powder; stir into the cocoa mixture. Stir in vanilla and cookie crumbs.

Pour into a greased 11-in. x 7-in. x 2-in. baking pan. Spoon cream cheese mixture over batter; cut through batter with a knife to swirl. Bake at 350° for 25-30 minutes or until a toothpick inserted near the center comes out with moist crumbs. Cool completely. **Yield:** 2 dozen.

Cookie Dough Brownies

When I take these rich brownies to any get-to-gether, I carry the recipe, too, because it always gets requested. Children of all ages love the cookie dough filling. —Wendy Bailey, Elida, Ohio

    2 cups sugar
1-1/2 cups all-purpose flour
    1/2 cup baking cocoa
    1/2 teaspoon salt
      1 cup vegetable oil
      4 eggs
      2 teaspoons vanilla extract
    1/2 cup chopped walnuts, optional
FILLING:
    1/2 cup butter, softened
    1/2 cup packed brown sugar
    1/4 cup sugar
      2 tablespoons milk
      1 teaspoon vanilla extract
      1 cup all-purpose flour
GLAZE:
      1 cup (6 ounces) semisweet chocolate
        chips
      1 tablespoon shortening
    3/4 cup chopped walnuts

In a mixing bowl, combine sugar, flour, cocoa and salt. Add oil, eggs and vanilla; beat at medium speed for 3 minutes. Stir in walnuts if desired. Pour into a greased 13-in. x 9-in. x 2-in. baking pan. Bake at 350° for 30 minutes or until brownies test done. Cool completely.

For filling, cream butter and sugars in a mixing bowl. Add milk and vanilla; mix well. Beat in flour. Spread over the brownies; chill until firm. For glaze, melt chocolate chips and shortening in a saucepan, stirring until smooth. Spread over filling. Immediately sprinkle with nuts, pressing down slightly. **Yield:** 3 dozen.

Snow Flurry Brownies

These brownies are the best dessert in my recipe box. I've even prepared them on the spur of the moment while company was over for dinner. They take just minutes to mix up, are out of the oven in half an hour and generate many compliments.
—Sherry Olson, Boulder, Colorado

      1 cup sugar
    1/2 cup butter, melted
      2 eggs
    1/2 teaspoon vanilla extract
    2/3 cup all-purpose flour
    1/2 cup baking cocoa
    1/2 teaspoon baking powder
    1/2 teaspoon salt
    1/2 cup vanilla or white chips
    1/2 cup chopped macadamia nuts or
        chopped almonds

In a bowl, whisk together sugar, butter, eggs and vanilla. Combine flour, cocoa, baking powder and salt; add to sugar mixture and mix well. Stir in vanilla chips and nuts.

Spread into a greased 8-in. square baking pan. Bake at 350° for 25-30 minutes or until a toothpick inserted near the center comes out with moist crumbs (do not overbake). Cool on a wire rack. Cut into diamond shapes if desired. **Yield:** 16 brownies.

Chocolate Maple Bars

My family runs a maple syrup operation, and I'm always looking for new ways to incorporate maple syrup into my cooking and baking. These bars are delicious!

—Cathy Schumacher, Alto, Michigan

    1/2 cup shortening
    3/4 cup maple syrup
    1/2 cup sugar
      3 eggs
      3 tablespoons milk
      1 teaspoon vanilla extract
1-1/4 cups all-purpose flour
    1/4 teaspoon baking powder
    1/4 teaspoon salt
1-1/2 squares (1-1/2 ounces) unsweetened
        chocolate,
        melted
    1/2 cup chopped pecans
    1/2 cup flaked coconut
FROSTING:
    1/4 cup butter or margarine, softened
      1 cup confectioners' sugar
    1/2 cup baking cocoa
    1/2 cup maple syrup
      1 cup miniature marshmallows

In a mixing bowl, cream the shortening, syrup and sugar. Beat in the eggs, milk and vanilla. Combine the flour, baking powder and salt; add to creamed mixture and mix well. Remove half of the batter to another bowl.

Combine melted chocolate and pecans; stir into one bowl. Spread into a greased 13-in. x 9-in. x 2-in. baking pan. Add coconut to remaining batter. Spread carefully over chocolate batter. Bake at 350° for 25 minutes or until a toothpick inserted near the center comes out clean. Cool completely on a wire rack.

For frosting, in a small mixing bowl, cream butter. Gradually add confectioners' sugar and cocoa. Slowly add syrup, beating until smooth. Fold in marshmallows. Frost bars. **Yield:** 3 dozen.

Cranberry Date Bars

I first discovered this recipe at Christmas, but it's a great way to use frozen cranberries throughout the year. I help out at the school our three sons attend and am active at our church. It seems I'm always baking a batch of these moist bars for some event. —Bonnie Nieter, Warsaw, Indiana

      1 package (12 ounces) fresh or frozen
        cranberries, thawed
      1 package (8 ounces) chopped dates
      2 tablespoons water
      1 teaspoon vanilla extract
      2 cups all-purpose flour
      2 cups old-fashioned oats
1-1/2 cups packed brown sugar
    1/2 teaspoon baking soda
    1/2 teaspoon salt
      1 cup butter, melted
GLAZE:
      2 cups confectioners' sugar
      2 to 3 tablespoons orange juice
    1/2 teaspoon vanilla extract

In a covered saucepan over low heat, simmer cranberries, dates and water for 15 minutes, stirring occasionally until the cranberries have popped. Remove from the heat; stir in vanilla and set aside.

In a large bowl, combine the flour, oats, brown sugar, baking soda and salt. Stir in butter until well blended. Pat half into an ungreased 13-in. x 9-in. x 2-in. baking pan. Bake at 350° for 8 minutes.

Spoon cranberry mixture over crust. Sprinkle with the remaining oat mixture. Pat gently. Bake at 350° for 25-30 minutes or until browned. Cool. Combine glaze ingredients; drizzle over bars. **Yield:** 3 dozen.

Cookies

Chocolate Malted Cookies, p. 24

Chocolate Malted Cookies

The only thing more comforting than a cookie warm from the oven is two cookies! And speaking of more, no recipe contest has ever stirred up more excitement than our Cookie Collection contest—with 13,000 entries in all.

Cookie lovers shared favorite recipes for cookies and bars of all kinds. Our food editors spent weeks sorting through the mountain of entries; then our Test Kitchen staff began baking. Our panel of judges had the tasty job of picking the winners.

At the top of the cookie jar is Grand Prize Winner Chocolate Malted Cookies from Teri Rasey-Bolf, who says, "These are the next best thing to good old-fashioned malted milk. With malted milk powder, chocolate syrup plus chocolate chips and chunks, these are the best cookies I've ever tasted!"

—Teri Rasey-Bolf of Cadillac, Michigan

> 1 cup butter-flavored shortening
> 1-1/4 cups packed brown sugar
> 1/2 cup malted milk powder
> 2 tablespoons chocolate syrup
> 1 tablespoon vanilla extract
> 1 egg
> 2 cups all-purpose flour
> 1 teaspoon baking soda
> 1/2 teaspoon salt
> 1-1/2 cups semisweet chocolate chunks
> 1 cup (6 ounces) milk chocolate chips

In a mixing bowl, combine the first five ingredients; beat for 2 minutes. Add egg. Combine the flour, baking soda and salt; gradually add to the creamed mixture, mixing well after each addition. Stir in chocolate chunks and chips.

Shape into 2-in. balls; place 3 in. apart on ungreased baking sheets. Bake at 375° for 12-14 minutes or until golden brown. Cool for 2 minutes before removing to a wire rack. **Yield:** about 1-1/2 dozen.

Spice Cookies with Pumpkin Dip

My husband and kids eat the first dozen of these cookies, warm from the oven, before the next tray is even done.

—Kelly McNeal, Derby, Kansas

> 1-1/2 cups butter, softened
> 2 cups sugar
> 2 eggs
> 1/2 cup molasses
> 4 cups all-purpose flour
> 4 teaspoons baking soda
> 2 teaspoons ground cinnamon
> 1 teaspoon each ground ginger and cloves
> 1 teaspoon salt
> Additional sugar
> PUMPKIN DIP:
> 1 package (8 ounces) cream cheese, softened
> 1 can (18 ounces) pumpkin pie mix
> 2 cups confectioners' sugar
> 1/2 to 1 teaspoon ground cinnamon
> 1/4 to 1/2 teaspoon ground ginger

In a mixing bowl, cream butter and sugar. Add eggs, one at a time, beating well after each addition. Add molasses; mix well. Combine the flour, baking soda, cinnamon, ginger, cloves and salt; add to creamed mixture and mix well. Chill overnight.

Shape into 1/2-in. balls; roll in sugar. Place 2 in. apart on ungreased baking sheets. Bake at 375° for 6 minutes or until edges begin to brown. Cool for 2 minutes before removing to a wire rack.

For dip, beat cream cheese in a mixing bowl until smooth. Add pumpkin pie mix; beat well. Add sugar, cinnamon and ginger; beat until smooth. Serve with cookies. Store leftover dip in the refrigerator. **Yield:** about 20 dozen (3 cups dip).

Coconut Washboards

*I've been making my husband these favorite cook-
ies most of the years we've been married. Our
great-grandchildren like to come over to munch
on these chewy treats, too.*
—*Tommie Sue Shaw, McAlester, Oklahoma*

      1/2 cup butter, softened
      1/2 cup shortening
        2 cups packed brown sugar
        2 eggs
      1/4 cup water
        1 teaspoon vanilla extract
        4 cups all-purpose flour
    1-1/2 teaspoons baking powder
      1/2 teaspoon baking soda
      1/4 teaspoon salt
        1 cup flaked coconut

In a mixing bowl, cream the butter, shortening and
sugar for 2 minutes or until fluffy. Add eggs; mix
well. Gradually add water and vanilla; mix well.
Combine flour, baking powder, baking soda and
salt; add to the creamed mixture. Fold in coconut.
Cover and refrigerate for 2-4 hours.

Shape into 1-in. balls. Place 2 in. apart on
greased baking sheets; flatten with fingers into
2-1/2-in. x 1-in. oblong shapes. Press lengthwise
with a floured fork. Bake at 400° for 8-10 minutes
or until lightly browned. Cool 2 minutes before
removing to a wire rack. **Yield:** about 9 dozen.

Lemon Butter Cookies

*These tender cutout cookies have a slight lemon
flavor that makes them stand out from the rest.
They're very easy to roll out compared to other
sugar cookies I've worked with. I know you'll enjoy them as much as we do.*
—*Judy McCreight, Springfield, Illinois*

        1 cup butter, softened
        2 cups sugar
        2 eggs, beaten
      1/4 cup milk
        2 teaspoons lemon extract
      1/2 teaspoon salt
    4-1/2 cups all-purpose flour
        2 teaspoons baking powder
      1/4 teaspoon baking soda
Colored sugar, optional

In a mixing bowl, cream the butter and sugar. Add
the eggs, milk and lemon extract. Combine dry
ingredients; gradually add to creamed mixture.
Cover and chill for 2 hours.

Roll out on a lightly floured surface to 1/8-in.
thickness. Cut with a 2-in. cookie cutter dipped in
flour. Place 2 in. apart on ungreased baking sheets.
Sprinkle with colored sugar if desired.

Bake at 350° for 8-9 minutes or until the edges
just begin to brown. Remove to wire racks to cool.
Yield: about 13 dozen.

Rolled Oat Cookies

I like to keep some of this dough in the freezer at all times, since it's so handy to slice, bake and serve at a moment's notice. So they're the perfect cookie to serve drop-in guests or to take to bake sales or potluck suppers. These wholesome cookies are also super with a cup of coffee—in fact, we occasionally grab a few for breakfast when we're in a hurry.
—Kathi Peters, Chilliwack, British Columbia

- **1 cup butter**
- **1 cup packed brown sugar**
- **1/4 cup water**
- **1 teaspoon vanilla extract**
- **3 cups quick-cooking oats**
- **1-1/4 cups all-purpose flour**
- **1 teaspoon salt**
- **1/4 teaspoon baking soda**

In a mixing bowl, cream the butter and sugar. Add the water and vanilla; mix well. Combine the dry ingredients; add to creamed mixture and mix well. Chill for 30 minutes.

Shape dough into two 1-1/2-in. rolls; wrap tightly in waxed paper. Chill for 2 hours or until firm. Cut into 1/2-in. slices and place 2 in. apart on greased baking sheets. Bake at 375° for 12 minutes or until lightly browned. Remove cookies to wire racks to cool. **Yield:** about 3-1/2 dozen.

Peanut Butter Sandwich Cookies

I work in our school office and help my husband on our hog and cattle farm. When I find time to bake a treat, I like it to be special. The creamy filling gives traditional peanut butter cookies a new twist.
—Debbie Kokes, Tabor, South Dakota

- **1 cup butter-flavored shortening**
- **1 cup creamy peanut butter**
- **1 cup sugar**
- **1 cup packed brown sugar**
- **1 teaspoon vanilla extract**
- **3 eggs**
- **3 cups all-purpose flour**
- **2 teaspoons baking soda**
- **1/4 teaspoon salt**
FILLING:
- **1/2 cup creamy peanut butter**
- **3 cups confectioners' sugar**
- **1 teaspoon vanilla extract**
- **5 to 6 tablespoons milk**

In a mixing bowl, cream the shortening, peanut butter and sugars. Add vanilla. Add eggs, one at a time, beating well after each addition. Combine flour, baking soda and salt; add to creamed mixture.

Shape into 1-in. balls and place 2 in. apart on ungreased baking sheets. Flatten to 3/8-in. thickness with a fork. Bake at 375° for 7-8 minutes or until golden. Cool on wire racks.

In a mixing bowl, beat filling ingredients until smooth. Spread on half of the cookies and top each with another cookie. **Yield:** about 4 dozen.

Frosted Ginger Cookies

My husband and I just built a new house in a small rural community in western New York. I work all day in an office, and I enjoy baking in the evening to relax. The wonderful aroma of these soft, delicious cookies in our oven has made our new house smell like home.
—Jeanne Matteson, South Dayton, New York

1-1/2 cups butter
   1 cup sugar
   1 cup packed brown sugar
   2 eggs
  1/2 cup molasses
   2 teaspoons vanilla extract
4-1/2 cups all-purpose flour
   1 tablespoon ground ginger
   2 teaspoons baking soda
   2 teaspoons ground cinnamon
  1/2 teaspoon salt
  1/2 teaspoon ground cloves
FROSTING:
  1/3 cup packed brown sugar
  1/4 cup milk
   2 tablespoons butter
   2 cups confectioners' sugar
  1/2 teaspoon vanilla extract or caramel
     flavoring
Pinch salt

In a mixing bowl, cream butter and sugars. Add the eggs, one at a time, beating well after each addition. Stir in molasses and vanilla; mix well. Combine dry ingredients; gradually add to creamed mixture. Drop by tablespoonfuls 2 in. apart onto ungreased baking sheets. Bake at 325° for 12-15 minutes or until cookies spring back when touched lightly (do not overbake). Remove to wire racks.

For frosting, in a medium saucepan, bring brown sugar, milk and butter to a boil; boil for 1 minute, stirring constantly. Remove from the heat (mixture will look curdled at first). Cool for 3 minutes. Add confectioners' sugar, vanilla and salt; mix well. Frost warm cookies. **Yield:** about 6 dozen.

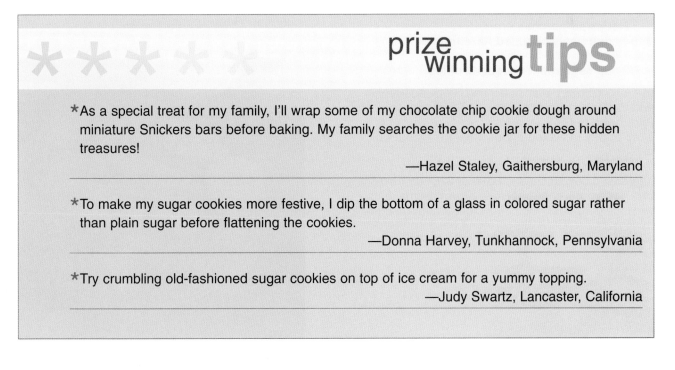

prize winning tips

*As a special treat for my family, I'll wrap some of my chocolate chip cookie dough around miniature Snickers bars before baking. My family searches the cookie jar for these hidden treasures!
—Hazel Staley, Gaithersburg, Maryland

*To make my sugar cookies more festive, I dip the bottom of a glass in colored sugar rather than plain sugar before flattening the cookies.
—Donna Harvey, Tunkhannock, Pennsylvania

*Try crumbling old-fashioned sugar cookies on top of ice cream for a yummy topping.
—Judy Swartz, Lancaster, California

Hazelnut Shortbread

We have several acres of hazelnut trees here in the Willamette Valley, where the climate is perfect for this crop. Harvesttime is a big family event with everyone pitching in to help. I try to incorporate this wonderful nut into our recipes, and this cookie is always a hit.

—Karen Morrell, Canby, Oregon

    1 cup butter, softened
  1/2 cup sugar
    2 tablespoons maple syrup or honey
    2 teaspoons vanilla extract
    2 cups all-purpose flour
1-1/4 cups finely chopped hazelnuts or
      filberts
  1/2 cup semisweet chocolate chips

In a mixing bowl, cream butter and sugar. Add syrup and vanilla. Add flour and mix just until combined; fold in the nuts. Shape into two 1-1/2-in. rolls; wrap tightly in waxed paper. Chill for 2 hours or until firm.

Cut into 1/4-in. slices and place 2 in. apart on ungreased baking sheets. Bake at 325° for 14-16 minutes or until edges begin to brown. Remove to wire racks to cool. Melt chocolate chips; drizzle over cookies. Allow chocolate to harden. **Yield:** about 6 dozen.

Chocolaty Double Crunchers

I first tried these fun crispy cookies at a family picnic when I was a child. Packed with oats, cornflakes and coconut, they quickly became a "regular" at our house.

—Cheryl Johnson, Upper Marlboro, Maryland

  1/2 cup butter, softened
  1/2 cup sugar
  1/2 cup packed brown sugar
    1 egg
  1/2 teaspoon vanilla extract
    1 cup all-purpose flour
  1/2 teaspoon baking soda
  1/4 teaspoon salt
    1 cup quick-cooking oats
    1 cup crushed cornflakes
  1/2 cup flaked coconut
FILLING:
    2 packages (3 ounces each) cream
      cheese, softened
1-1/2 cups confectioners' sugar
    2 cups (12 ounces) semisweet chocolate
      chips, melted

In a mixing bowl, cream butter and sugars. Add egg and vanilla; mix well. Combine flour, baking soda and salt; add to creamed mixture and mix well. Add oats, cornflakes and coconut.

Shape into 1-in. balls and place 2 in. apart on greased baking sheets. Flatten with a glass dipped lightly in flour. Bake at 350° for 8-10 minutes or until lightly browned. Remove to wire racks to cool.

For filling, beat cream cheese and sugar until smooth. Add the chocolate; mix well. Spread about 1 tablespoon on the bottom of half of the cookies and top each with another cookie. Store in the refrigerator. **Yield:** about 2 dozen.

Cakes &
Tortes

Cherry Cream Torte, p. 35

Strawberry Custard Torte

(Pictured below)

This elegant dessert is as beautiful as it is delicious. Not only is it ultra-easy to prepare, but it's a make-ahead recipe, so there's no last-minute fussing when company is coming. —Brenda Bodnar Euclid, Ohio

> 1 package (18-1/4 ounces) yellow cake mix
> 1/3 cup sugar
> 1 tablespoon cornstarch
> 1/8 teaspoon salt
> 1 cup milk
> 2 egg yolks, lightly beaten
> 1 tablespoon butter
> 1 teaspoon vanilla extract
> 1 carton (8 ounces) frozen whipped topping, thawed
> 1 package (12 ounces) frozen sweetened sliced strawberries, thawed and drained
> Sliced fresh strawberries and mint leaves, optional

Prepare and bake cake according to package directions, using two greased and floured 9-in. round baking pans. Cool for 10 minutes; remove from pans to wire racks to cool completely.

In a saucepan, combine the sugar, cornstarch and salt; gradually stir in milk until smooth. Bring to a boil over medium heat; cook and stir for 2 minutes or until thickened. Remove from the heat. Stir a small amount of hot filling into egg yolks; return all to pan, stirring constantly. Bring to a gentle boil; cook and stir for 2 minutes. Remove from the heat. Stir in butter and vanilla. Cover and refrigerate until chilled.

Place half of the whipped topping in a bowl; add strawberries. Split each cake into two horizontal layers; place one layer on a serving plate. Spread with half of the strawberry mixture. Top with a second cake layer; spread with custard. Add third layer; spread with remaining strawberry mixture. Top with remaining cake and whipped topping. Refrigerate overnight. Garnish with strawberries and mint if desired. **Yield:** 12 servings.

Peach Upside-Down Cake

Peaches and coconut give this cake a refreshing flavor that's especially nice for spring and summer. —Terri Holmgren, Swanville, Minnesota

> 1/3 cup butter, melted
> 1/2 cup packed brown sugar
> 1 can (29 ounces) peach halves
> 1/4 cup flaked coconut
> 2 eggs
> 2/3 cup sugar
> 1/2 teaspoon almond extract
> 1 cup all-purpose flour
> 1 teaspoon baking powder
> 1/4 teaspoon salt

Pour butter into a 9-in. round baking pan; sprinkle with brown sugar. Drain peaches, reserving 6 tablespoons of syrup. Arrange peach halves, cut side down, in a single layer over the sugar. Sprinkle coconut around peaches; set aside.

In a mixing bowl, beat eggs until thick and lemon-colored; gradually beat in sugar. Add extract and reserved syrup. Combine flour, baking powder and salt; add to egg mixture and mix well. Pour over peaches.

Bake at 350° for 50-60 minutes or until a toothpick inserted near the center comes out clean. Cool for 10 minutes; invert cake onto a serving plate. Serve warm. **Yield:** 6-8 servings.

Almond Brittle Torte

I brought this impressive cake to my bridge club potluck—and now they want it every time we meet. Homemade brittle makes it extra special. —Marrian Storm, Athol, Idaho

1-1/2 cups sugar
  1/2 cup water
  1/2 cup light corn syrup
  1/4 teaspoon instant coffee granules
    3 teaspoons baking soda
    1 cup slivered almonds
CAKE:
    8 eggs, *separated*
  1/4 cup water
    3 teaspoons lemon juice
    1 teaspoon vanilla extract
1-1/2 cups cake flour
1-1/2 cups sugar, *divided*
    1 teaspoon cream of tartar
    1 teaspoon salt
3-1/2 cups heavy whipping cream, whipped

Line a 13-in. x 9-in. x 2-in. baking pan with foil; butter the foil and set aside. In a saucepan, combine the sugar, water, corn syrup and coffee granules. Bring to a boil over medium-high heat, stirring constantly, until a candy thermometer reads 290°. Sprinkle with baking soda, stirring constantly (mixture will foam). Stir in the almonds. Pour into prepared pan. Cool completely.

In a large mixing bowl, combine the egg yolks, water, lemon juice and vanilla; mix well. Combine flour and 3/4 cup sugar; add to egg yolk mixture and mix well. In a small mixing bowl, beat egg whites, cream of tartar and salt until soft peaks form. Beat in remaining sugar, 1 tablespoon at a time. Fold into the batter. Pour into an ungreased 10-in. tube pan. Bake at 350° for 50-55 minutes or until cake springs back when lightly touched. Cool on a wire rack.

Remove cake from pan. Split horizontally into four layers. Place bottom layer on a serving plate; spread with about 3/4 cup whipped cream. Break almond brittle into small pieces; sprinkle some over cream. Repeat layers twice. Spread remaining whipped cream over top and sides of cake; sprinkle with remaining brittle. Refrigerate until serving. **Yield:** 12-16 servings.

Editor's Note: Almond brittle will melt on the whipped cream and form a syrup.

Zucchini Cake

(Pictured above right)

What gardener doesn't have extra zucchini? When it's abundant, I shred and freeze plenty so I have it on hand to bake this moist sheet cake all year long. The cream cheese frosting is yummy.
    —Marie Hoyer, Hodgenville, Kentucky

2-1/2 cups all-purpose flour
    2 cups sugar

1-1/2 teaspoons ground cinnamon
    1 teaspoon salt
  1/2 teaspoon baking powder
  1/2 teaspoon baking soda
    1 cup vegetable oil
    4 eggs
    2 cups shredded zucchini
  1/2 cup chopped walnuts, optional
FROSTING:
    1 package (3 ounces) cream cheese, softened
  1/4 cup butter, softened
    1 tablespoon milk
    1 teaspoon vanilla extract
    2 cups confectioners' sugar
Additional chopped walnuts, optional

In a mixing bowl, combine flour, sugar, cinnamon, salt, baking powder and baking soda. Combine oil and eggs; add to dry ingredients and mix well. Add zucchini; stir until thoroughly combined. Fold in walnuts if desired.

Pour into a greased 13-in. x 9-in. x 2-in. baking pan. Bake at 350° for 35-40 minutes or until a toothpick inserted near the center comes out clean. Cool.

For frosting, in a small mixing bowl, beat cream cheese, butter, milk and vanilla until smooth. Add confectioners' sugar and mix well. Frost cake. Sprinkle with nuts if desired. Store in the refrigerator. **Yield:** 20-24 servings.

Editor's Note: If using frozen blueberries, do not thaw before adding to batter.

Upside-Down German Chocolate Cake

This simple recipe yields a delectable German chocolate cake that folks will "flip over"! The tempting coconut and pecan "frosting" bakes under the batter and ends up on top when you turn the cake out of the pan.
—Mrs. Harold Sanders
Glouster, Ohio

    1/2 cup packed brown sugar
    1/4 cup butter
    2/3 cup pecan halves
    2/3 cup flaked coconut
    1/4 cup evaporated milk
CAKE:
    1/3 cup butter, softened
    1 cup sugar
    1 package (4 ounces) German sweet chocolate, melted
    2 eggs
    1 teaspoon vanilla extract
1-1/2 cups all-purpose flour
    1/2 teaspoon baking soda
    1/2 teaspoon baking powder
    1/2 teaspoon salt
    3/4 cup buttermilk
Whipped topping, optional

In a saucepan over low heat, cook and stir brown sugar and butter until sugar is dissolved and butter is melted. Spread into a greased 9-in. square baking pan. Sprinkle with pecans and coconut. Drizzle with evaporated milk; set aside.

    In a mixing bowl, cream butter and sugar. Beat in chocolate, eggs and vanilla. Combine dry ingredients; add to creamed mixture alternately with buttermilk. Pour over topping in pan. Bake at 350° for 40-45 minutes or until a toothpick inserted near center comes out clean. Cool for 5 minutes before inverting onto a serving plate. Serve with whipped topping if desired. **Yield:** 9 servings.

Blueberry Buckle

(Pictured above)

I used to buy baskets of blueberries from a man who had numerous bushes. One of my co-workers gave me this recipe, and it's become a favorite.
—Helen Dodge, Meriden, Connecticut

    1/4 cup shortening
    3/4 cup sugar
    1 egg
    2 cups all-purpose flour
    2 teaspoons baking powder
    1/2 teaspoon salt
    1/2 cup milk
    2 cups fresh *or* frozen blueberries
TOPPING:
    1/2 cup sugar
    1/3 cup all-purpose flour
    1/2 teaspoon ground cinnamon
    1/4 cup cold butter

In a mixing bowl, cream the shortening and sugar. Beat in egg; mix well. Combine the flour, baking powder and salt; add alternately to creamed mixture with milk. Fold in blueberries. Pour into a greased 9-in. square baking dish.

    For topping, combine the sugar, flour and cinnamon; cut in butter until mixture resembles coarse crumbs. Sprinkle over batter. Bake at 350° for 40-45 minutes or until a toothpick inserted near the center comes clean. Cool for 10 minutes before cutting. Serve warm or cooled. **Yield:** 9 servings.

Orange Chiffon Cake

This cake recipe was given to me by my sister-in-law many years ago. It's deliciously light in texture, compatible with any meal and makes a beautiful presentation for special occasions.
—Ann Pitt, Mountainside, New Jersey

Dessert Lovers Cookbook

2 cups all-purpose flour
1-1/2 cups sugar
   3 teaspoons baking powder
   1/4 teaspoon salt
   7 eggs, *separated*
   1/2 cup orange juice
   1/2 cup vegetable oil
   1/4 cup water
   2 teaspoons vanilla extract
   1 tablespoon grated orange peel
   2 teaspoons grated lemon peel
   1/2 teaspoon cream of tartar

ICING:
   1/2 cup confectioners' sugar
   2 tablespoons shortening
   1 tablespoon butter, softened
   1 can (8 ounces) crushed pineapple, well
     drained

Sift the flour, sugar, baking powder and salt into a large bowl; make a well in the center. In another bowl, beat egg yolks until thick and lemon-colored. Beat in the orange juice, oil, water, vanilla, and orange and lemon peels. Pour into well in dry ingredients; beat with a wooden spoon until smooth. In a mixing bowl, beat egg whites on medium speed until foamy. Add cream of tartar; beat until stiff peaks form. Gradually fold into batter.

Transfer to an ungreased 10-in. tube pan. Bake at 325° for 55-60 minutes or until cake springs back when lightly touched. Immediately invert cake; cool completely. Loosen cake from sides of pan; remove cake and place on a serving platter.

For icing, combine the confectioners' sugar, shortening and butter until smooth. Spread over the top of the cake. Spoon pineapple over the icing. **Yield:** 12 servings.

Chocolate Cookie Torte

(Pictured at right)

This recipe has been used many times in our family for get-togethers. It's easy to make, a nice change from the more traditional cakes served at parties and beautiful when served. —Irene Bigler
New Cumberland, Pennsylvania

   1/2 cup butter, softened
   1 cup sugar
   1 egg
   1 egg yolk
   1/2 teaspoon vanilla extract
   2 cups all-purpose flour
   1 teaspoon baking powder
   1/2 teaspoon salt
Additional sugar

FROSTING:
   2 cups (12 ounces) semisweet chocolate
     chips
   1/2 cup half-and-half cream
   2 cups heavy whipping cream, whipped
   2 teaspoons vanilla extract
Chocolate sprinkles

In a mixing bowl, cream butter and sugar. Beat in the egg, yolk and vanilla. Combine flour, baking powder and salt; gradually add to the creamed mixture and mix well. Form into a long log; cut into eight equal pieces. Shape each into a ball; wrap in plastic wrap. Refrigerate for 1 hour.

Roll balls in additional sugar; place between two sheets of waxed paper. Roll each into a 6-in. circle. Remove top sheet of waxed paper; flip the circles onto ungreased baking sheets. Remove waxed paper; prick dough with a fork. Bake at 350° for 10-12 minutes or until lightly browned. Carefully loosen cookies and cool on paper towels.

For frosting, melt chocolate chips with half-and-half in a heavy saucepan, stirring occasionally. Cool. Combine whipped cream and vanilla; fold into chocolate mixture. Layer cookies, spreading 1/4 cup frosting between each layer. Spread remaining frosting over sides and top. Decorate with chocolate sprinkles. Refrigerate overnight before cutting. **Yield:** 8-10 servings.

Old-Fashioned Carrot Cake

(Pictured below)

A pleasingly moist cake, this treat is the one I requested that my mom make each year for my birthday. It's dotted with sweet carrots and a hint of cinnamon. The fluffy buttery frosting is scrumptious with chopped walnuts stirred in. One piece of this cake is never enough!
—Kim Orr
Louisville, Kentucky

      4 eggs
      2 cups sugar
1-1/2 cups vegetable oil
      2 cups all-purpose flour
      2 to 3 teaspoons ground cinnamon
      1 teaspoon baking powder
      1 teaspoon baking soda
   1/4 teaspoon salt
   1/4 teaspoon ground nutmeg
      2 cups grated carrots
FROSTING:
   1/2 cup butter, softened
      1 package (3 ounces) cream cheese,
         softened
3-3/4 cups confectioners' sugar
      1 teaspoon vanilla extract
      2 to 3 tablespoons milk
      1 cup chopped walnuts
Carrot curls and additional walnuts, optional

In a mixing bowl, combine eggs, sugar and oil; mix well. Combine flour, cinnamon, baking powder, baking soda, salt and nutmeg; beat into egg mixture. Stir in carrots. Pour into two greased and floured 9-in. round baking pans.

Bake at 350° for 35-40 minutes or until a toothpick inserted near the center comes out clean. Cool for 10 minutes before removing from pans to wire racks.

For frosting, in a mixing bowl, cream butter and cream cheese. Gradually beat in confectioners' sugar and vanilla. Add enough milk to achieve desired spreading consistency. Stir in walnuts.

Spread frosting between layers and over top and sides of cake. Garnish with carrot curls and walnuts if desired. Refrigerate leftovers. **Yield:** 12 servings.

Walnut Blitz Torte

This pretty torte is very popular at family gatherings. Everyone always asks for the recipe.
—Suzan Stacey, Parsonsfield, Maine

      2 tablespoons sugar
4-1/2 teaspoons cornstarch
      1 egg yolk
      1 cup milk
      1 teaspoon vanilla extract
CAKE BATTER:
   1/2 cup butter, softened
   1/2 cup sugar
      4 egg yolks
      1 teaspoon vanilla extract
      1 cup all-purpose flour
      1 teaspoon baking powder
   1/4 teaspoon salt
      5 tablespoons milk
MERINGUE:
      5 egg whites
      1 cup sugar
      2 cups chopped walnuts, *divided*

In a saucepan, combine sugar and cornstarch. Combine egg yolk and milk; add to pan. Bring to a gentle boil over medium-low heat, stirring constantly. Cook and stir for 2 minutes. Remove from the heat; stir in vanilla. Cover and refrigerate.

Meanwhile, in a mixing bowl, cream the butter and sugar. Add egg yolks and vanilla; mix well. Combine flour, baking powder and salt; add to creamed mixture alternately with milk. Spread into two greased and floured 9-in. round baking pans; set aside.

In a small mixing bowl, beat egg whites on medium speed until foamy. Gradually beat in sugar, 1 tablespoon at a time, on high until stiff glossy peaks form and sugar is dissolved. Fold in 1 cup nuts. Spread meringue evenly over batter. Sprinkle with remaining nuts. Bake at 325° for 35-40 minutes or until meringue is browned and crisp. Cool on wire

racks for 10 minutes (meringue will crack). Carefully run a knife around edge of pans to loosen. Remove to wire racks; cool with meringue side up.

To assemble, place one cake with meringue side up on a serving plate; carefully spread with custard. Top with remaining cake. Refrigerate until serving. **Yield:** 12-16 servings.

Cherry Cream Torte

(Pictured on page 29)

When you set this gorgeous dessert on the table, your guests will sing your praises. You're the only one who has to know how simple it is to prepare.
—Mary Anne McWhirter, Pearland, Texas

2 packages (3 ounces *each***) ladyfingers**
2 tablespoons white grape *or* **apple juice**
1 package (8 ounces) cream cheese,
    softened
2/3 cup sugar
1 teaspoon almond extract, *divided*
2 cups heavy whipping cream, whipped
1 can (21 ounces) cherry pie filling
Toasted sliced almonds and additional
    whipped cream, optional

Split ladyfingers lengthwise; brush with juice. Place a layer of ladyfingers around the sides and over the bottom of a lightly greased 9-in. springform pan.

In a mixing bowl, beat cream cheese until smooth; add sugar and 1/2 teaspoon extract. Beat on medium for 1 minute. Fold in whipped cream. Spread half over crust. Arrange remaining ladyfingers in a spoke-like fashion. Spread evenly with the remaining cream cheese mixture. Cover and chill overnight.

Combine the pie filling and remaining extract; spread over the cream cheese layer. Chill for at least 2 hours. To serve, remove sides of pan. Garnish with almonds and whipped cream if desired. **Yield:** 16-18 servings.

Chocolate Cake Roll

(Pictured above right)

This delectable dessert features sweet whipped cream and moist chocolate cake rolled up and dusted with confectioners' sugar. A family favorite, it winds up any special meal in festive fashion.
—Cris O'Brien, Virginia Beach, Virginia

6 eggs, *separated*
1 cup sugar, *divided*

1 teaspoon vanilla extract
1/4 cup all-purpose flour
1/4 cup baking cocoa
1/4 teaspoon salt
1/2 teaspoon cream of tartar
1-1/2 cups heavy whipping cream
2 tablespoons confectioners' sugar
Additional confectioners' sugar

Place egg whites in a small mixing bowl; let stand at room temperature for 30 minutes. In a large mixing bowl, beat egg yolks on high speed until light and fluffy. Gradually add 1/2 cup sugar, beating until thick and lemon-colored. Stir in vanilla. Combine the flour, cocoa and salt; add to egg yolk mixture until blended.

Beat egg whites on medium until foamy. Add cream of tartar; beat until soft peaks form. Gradually add remaining sugar, 1 tablespoon at a time, beating on high until stiff peaks form. Stir a fourth of the egg white mixture into chocolate mixture. Fold in remaining egg white mixture until no egg white streaks remain.

Line a greased 15-in. x 10-in. x 1-in. baking pan with parchment paper; grease the paper. Spread batter evenly in pan. Bake at 350° for 12-15 minutes or until cake springs back when lightly touched in center (do not overbake). Cool for 5 minutes; invert onto a kitchen towel dusted with confectioners' sugar. Gently peel off parchment paper. Roll up cake in the towel jelly-roll style, starting with a short side. Cool completely on a wire rack.

In a mixing bowl, beat cream and confectioners' sugar until stiff peaks form; chill. Unroll cake; spread with whipped cream to within 1/2 in. of edges. Roll up again. Place seam side down on serving platter; chill. Dust with additional confectioners' sugar before serving. **Yield:** 12 servings.

whipped topping. Spread over cake. Sprinkle with pistachios. Refrigerate for about 30 minutes before cutting. Garnish with whole pistachios and mint if desired. Refrigerate leftovers. **Yield:** 12-15 servings.

Double Peanut Butter Cake

My family loves peanut butter, so a cake that has it in the batter and frosting is a big hit around our house. —Marie Hoyer, Hodgenville, Kentucky

- 1/2 cup creamy peanut butter
- 1/4 cup butter, softened
- 3/4 cup sugar
- 2 eggs
- 1-1/2 cups all-purpose flour
- 2 teaspoons baking powder
- 1/4 teaspoon salt
- 3/4 cup milk
- FROSTING:
- 1/3 cup chunky peanut butter
- 3 tablespoons butter, softened
- 3 cups confectioners' sugar
- 1/4 cup milk
- 1-1/2 teaspoons vanilla extract

In a mixing bowl, cream peanut butter, butter and sugar. Add eggs; mix well. Combine flour, baking powder and salt; add alternately with milk to creamed mixture. Mix well. Pour into a greased 9-in. square baking pan. Bake at 350° for 30-35 minutes or until a toothpick inserted near the center comes out clean. Cool on a wire rack.

For frosting, cream peanut butter and butter. Add sugar, milk and vanilla; mix until smooth. Frost cake. **Yield:** 9 servings.

Six-Layer Coconut Cake

I found this recipe when going through my grandmother's old files. It is simply the best. —Angela Leinenbach, Mechanicsville, Virginia

- 1 cup butter, softened
- 3 cups sugar
- 3 teaspoons vanilla extract
- 4 cups cake flour
- 1 teaspoon baking soda
- 1/2 teaspoon baking powder
- 1/2 teaspoon salt
- 2 cups buttermilk
- 6 egg whites
- FILLING:
- 1/2 cup sugar
- 2 tablespoons cornstarch

Pistachio Cake

(Pictured above)

Mom is well known for her holiday cookies, candies and cakes. This delicious dessert starts conveniently with a cake mix and instant pudding. You're sure to get requests for second helpings. —Becky Brunette, Minneapolis, Minnesota

- 1 package (18-1/4 ounces) white cake mix
- 1 package (3.4 ounces) instant pistachio pudding mix
- 1 cup lemon-lime soda
- 1 cup vegetable oil
- 3 eggs
- 1 cup chopped walnuts
- FROSTING:
- 1-1/2 cups cold milk
- 1 package (3.4 ounces) instant pistachio pudding mix
- 1 carton (8 ounces) frozen whipped topping, thawed
- 1/2 cup chopped pistachios, toasted
- Whole red shell pistachios and fresh mint, optional

In a mixing bowl, combine the first five ingredients. Beat on medium speed for 2 minutes; stir in walnuts. Pour into a greased 13-in. x 9-in. x 2-in. baking pan. Bake at 350° for 45-50 minutes or until a toothpick inserted near the center comes out clean. Cool on a wire rack.

For frosting, in a mixing bowl, beat milk and pudding mix on low speed for 2 minutes. Fold in the

1 cup orange juice
4 eggs, lightly beaten
1/4 cup butter
2 tablespoons grated orange peel
1 teaspoon orange extract
FROSTING:
1 cup sugar
2 egg whites
1/2 cup water
1/4 teaspoon salt
1/8 teaspoon cream of tartar
1/4 teaspoon vanilla extract
2 cups flaked coconut

In a mixing bowl, cream butter and sugar until light and fluffy. Add vanilla. Combine flour, baking soda, baking powder and salt; add to creamed mixture alternately with buttermilk. In another mixing bowl, beat egg whites until stiff peaks form; gently fold into batter. Pour into three greased and floured 9-in. round baking pans.

Bake at 350° for 25-30 minutes or until a toothpick comes out clean. Cool for 10 minutes; remove from pans to wire racks to cool completely.

In a saucepan, combine sugar and cornstarch. Gradually stir in orange juice until smooth. Bring to a boil; cook and stir for 2 minutes or until thickened. Remove from the heat. Gradually stir 1/2 cup into eggs; return all to pan, stirring constantly. Bring to a gentle boil; cook and stir for 2 minutes. Remove from the heat. Stir in butter, orange peel and extract. Cover and refrigerate.

In a heavy saucepan, combine sugar, egg whites, water, salt and cream of tartar. With a portable mixer, beat on low speed for 1 minute. Continue beating on low speed over low heat until frosting reaches 160°, about 12 minutes. Pour into a large mixing bowl; add vanilla. Beat on high until frosting forms stiff peaks, about 7 minutes.

Split each cake in half horizontally. Place one layer on a serving plate; spread with 1/3 cup filling. Repeat four times. Top with remaining cake layer. Spread frosting over top and sides. Sprinkle with coconut. Store in refrigerator. **Yield:** 12-14 servings.

Editor's Note: A stand mixer is recommended for beating the frosting after it reaches 160°.

Best Baking Pans

Use only the pan size recommended in the recipe. Dull aluminum baking pans are best for making cakes. They reflect heat away from the cake and give it a tender, light-brown crust.

Cool cakes for 10-15 minutes in the pan, unless the recipe directs otherwise. Loosen the cake by running a knife around the edge of the pan. Turn out onto a wire rack and cool completely.

Fudgy Raspberry Torte

(Pictured below)

Guests will think you fussed when you serve this three-layer torte made with convenient cake and pudding mixes, a bit of jam and fresh raspberries. It looks elegant for most any special occasion.
—Dolores Hurtt, Florence, Montana

1 package (18-1/4 ounces) chocolate
　fudge cake mix
1-1/3 cups water
3 eggs
1/3 cup vegetable oil
3/4 cup ground pecans
1-1/2 cups cold milk
1 package (3.9 ounces) instant chocolate
　fudge *or* chocolate pudding mix
1/2 cup seedless raspberry jam
1-1/2 cups whipped topping
1/4 cup finely chopped pecans
Fresh raspberries

In a mixing bowl, combine dry cake mix, water, eggs and oil. Add ground pecans; mix just until combined. Pour into three greased and floured 9-in. round baking pans. Bake at 350° for 15-20 minutes or until a toothpick inserted near the center comes out clean. Cool for 10 minutes before removing from pans to wire racks to cool completely.

In a mixing bowl, beat milk and pudding mix on low speed for 2 minutes or until thickened. In a saucepan, melt jam. Brush over the top of each cake. Place one cake on a serving plate; spread with half of the pudding. Repeat layers. Top with third cake layer; spread top with whipped topping. Sprinkle with chopped pecans. Garnish with raspberries. Store in the refrigerator. **Yield:** 12 servings.

Apple Pear Cake

When my sister Catherine made an apple cake for me, I asked her for the recipe. I made it a short time later and added some pears to the recipe.
—Mary Ann Lees, Centreville, Alabama

        2 cups shredded peeled apples
        2 cups shredded peeled pears
        2 cups sugar
    1-1/4 cups vegetable oil
        1 cup raisins
        1 cup chopped pecans
        2 eggs, beaten
        1 teaspoon vanilla extract
        3 cups all-purpose flour
        2 teaspoons baking soda
        2 teaspoons ground cinnamon
    1/2 teaspoon ground nutmeg
    1/2 teaspoon salt
CREAM CHEESE FROSTING:
        1 package (3 ounces) cream cheese,
            softened
    1/4 cup butter, softened
        3 cups confectioners' sugar
        2 tablespoons milk
    1/2 teaspoon vanilla extract

In a large bowl, combine the first eight ingredients. Combine dry ingredients; stir into the fruit mixture. Pour into a greased 13-in. x 9-in. x 2-in. baking pan. Bake at 325° for 1 hour or until a toothpick inserted near the center comes out clean. Cool on a wire rack.

For frosting, beat cream cheese and butter in a mixing bowl until fluffy. Add confectioners' sugar, milk and vanilla; mix well. Spread over cooled cake. Store in refrigerator. **Yield:** 12-15 servings.

Lemon Meringue Cake

This cake tastes just like lemon meringue pie! Fresh lemon flavor shines through in the custard filling, and the light meringue frosting adds a fancy finish. —Julie Courie, Macomb, Michigan

        1 package (18-1/4 ounces) lemon *or*
            yellow cake mix
        3 eggs
        1 cup water
    1/3 cup vegetable oil
FILLING:
        1 cup sugar
        3 tablespoons cornstarch
    1/4 teaspoon salt
    1/2 cup water
    1/4 cup lemon juice

        4 egg yolks, beaten
        4 teaspoons butter
        1 teaspoon grated lemon peel
MERINGUE:
        4 egg whites
    1/4 teaspoon cream of tartar
    3/4 cup sugar

In a mixing bowl, combine cake mix, eggs, water and oil. Beat on low until moistened. Beat on high for 2 minutes or until blended. Pour into two greased and floured 9-in. round baking pans. Bake at 350° for 25-30 minutes or until a toothpick inserted near the center comes out clean. Cool for 10 minutes; remove from pans to wire racks.

For filling, combine sugar, cornstarch and salt in a saucepan. Stir in water and juice until smooth. Bring to a boil over medium heat; cook and stir 1-2 minutes or until thickened. Remove from heat. Stir a small amount of hot filling into egg yolks; return all to pan, stirring constantly. Bring to a gentle boil; cook and stir for 2 minutes. Remove from heat; stir in butter and lemon peel. Cool completely.

For meringue, in a mixing bowl, beat egg whites and cream of tartar until foamy. Gradually beat in sugar on high until stiff peaks form. Split each cake into two layers. Place bottom layer on an oven-proof serving plate; spread with a third of the filling. Repeat layers twice. Top with fourth cake layer. Spread meringue over top and sides. Bake at 350° for 10-15 minutes or until meringue is lightly browned. Serve or refrigerate. **Yield:** 12-14 servings.

Gingerbread Cake

This dark moist cake combines the old-fashioned flavors of ginger and molasses. —Ila Alderman Galax, Virginia

    1/3 cup shortening
    1/2 cup sugar
        1 egg
    3/4 cup water
    1/2 cup molasses
    1-1/2 cups all-purpose flour
        1 teaspoon ground ginger
    1/2 teaspoon baking soda
    1/4 teaspoon salt
Whipped topping

In a mixing bowl, cream shortening and sugar. Beat in egg. Combine water and molasses. Combine the flour, ginger, baking soda and salt; add to creamed mixture alternately with molasses mixture. Pour into a greased 8-in. square baking pan.

Bake at 350° for 28-32 minutes or until a toothpick inserted near the center comes out clean. Serve warm with whipped topping. **Yield:** 9 servings.

Peanut Butter Chocolate Cake

In our chocolate-loving house, this snack cake disappears very quickly!
—Dorcas Yoder, Weyers Cave, Virginia

2 cups all-purpose flour
2 cups sugar
2/3 cup baking cocoa
2 teaspoons baking soda
1 teaspoon baking powder
1/2 teaspoon salt
2 eggs
1 cup milk
2/3 cup vegetable oil
1 teaspoon vanilla extract
1 cup brewed coffee, room temperature
PEANUT BUTTER FROSTING:
1 package (3 ounces) cream cheese, softened
1/4 cup creamy peanut butter
2 cups confectioners' sugar
2 tablespoons milk
1/2 teaspoon vanilla extract
Miniature semisweet chocolate chips, optional

In a mixing bowl, combine dry ingredients. Add eggs, milk, oil and vanilla; beat for 2 minutes. Stir in coffee (batter will be thin). Pour into a greased 13-in. x 9-in. x 2-in. baking pan. Bake at 350° for 35-40 minutes or until a toothpick inserted near the center comes out clean. Cool completely on a wire rack.

For frosting, beat cream cheese and peanut butter in a mixing bowl until smooth. Beat in sugar, milk and vanilla. Spread over cake. Sprinkle with chocolate chips if desired. Store in the refrigerator. **Yield:** 12-16 servings.

Pumpkin-Pecan Cake

I'm a full-time wife and mother who enjoys baking. This cake is a favorite.
—Joyce Platfoot, Wapakoneta, Ohio

2 cups crushed vanilla wafers (about 50)
1 cup chopped pecans
3/4 cup butter, softened
CAKE:
1 package (18-1/4 ounces) spice cake mix
1 can (16 ounces) solid-pack pumpkin
1/4 cup butter, softened
4 eggs
FILLING/TOPPING:
2/3 cup butter, softened
1 package (3 ounces) cream cheese, softened
3 cups confectioners' sugar
2 teaspoons vanilla extract
1/2 cup caramel ice cream topping
Pecan halves

In a mixing bowl on medium speed, beat the wafers, pecans and butter until crumbly, about 1 minute. Press into three greased and floured 9-in. round baking pans.

In another mixing bowl, beat cake mix, pumpkin, butter and eggs for 3 minutes. Spread over crust in each pan. Bake at 350° for 30 minutes or until a toothpick inserted near center comes out clean. Cool in pans 10 minutes; remove to wire racks and cool completely.

For filling, combine butter and cream cheese in a small mixing bowl. Add sugar and vanilla; beat on medium until light and fluffy, about 3 minutes. Thinly spread between layers (crumb side down) and on the sides of cake. Spread caramel topping over top of cake, allowing some to drip down the sides. Garnish with pecans. Store in the refrigerator. **Yield:** 16-20 servings.

Cranberry-Orange Pound Cake

This pretty pound cake is a favorite at the summer resort my husband and I operate.
—Sheree Swistun, Winnipeg, Manitoba

1-1/2 cups butter, softened
2-3/4 cups sugar
    6 eggs
    1 teaspoon vanilla extract
2-1/2 teaspoons grated orange peel
    3 cups all-purpose flour
    1 teaspoon baking powder
    1/2 teaspoon salt
    1 cup (8 ounces) sour cream
1-1/2 cups chopped fresh or frozen cranberries
VANILLA BUTTER SAUCE:
    1 cup sugar
    1 tablespoon all-purpose flour
    1/2 cup half-and-half cream
    1/2 cup butter, softened
    1/2 teaspoon vanilla extract

In a mixing bowl, cream butter. Gradually beat in sugar until light and fluffy, about 5-7 minutes. Add eggs, one at a time, beating well after each addition. Stir in vanilla and orange peel. Combine flour, baking powder and salt; add to the creamed mixture alternately with sour cream. Beat on low just until blended. Fold in cranberries. Pour into a greased and floured 10-in. fluted tube pan. Bake at 350° for 65-70 minutes or until a toothpick inserted near the center comes out clean. Cool in pan for 10 minutes; remove to a wire rack and cool completely.

In a small saucepan, combine sugar and flour. Stir in half-and-half and butter; bring to a boil over medium heat, stirring constantly. Boil for 2 minutes. Remove from the heat and stir in vanilla. Serve warm over cake. **Yield:** 16 servings (1-1/2 cups sauce).

Sunflower Potluck Cake

I wish I knew who to thank for the idea for my cake. I first saw it on the dessert table at a picnic. Later, for something different, I did my own variation.
—Lola Wiemer, Clarklake, Michigan

    3/4 cup butter, softened
1-2/3 cups sugar
    3 eggs
    1 teaspoon vanilla extract
    2 cups all-purpose flour
    2/3 cup baking cocoa
1-1/4 teaspoons baking soda
    1 teaspoon salt
    1/4 teaspoon baking powder
1-1/3 cups water
    1 cup prepared chocolate frosting, divided
    1 cup (6 ounces) semisweet chocolate chips
  22 cream-filled sponge cakes
    1 teaspoon milk

In a mixing bowl, cream butter and sugar. Add eggs, one at a time, beating well after each addition. Add vanilla. Combine dry ingredients; add to the creamed mixture alternately with water. Pour into two greased and floured 9-in. round baking pans. Bake at 350° for 25-30 minutes or until a toothpick inserted near the center comes out clean. Cool in pans for 10 minutes; remove to wire racks and cool completely. Freeze one layer for future use.

Set aside 1 tablespoon frosting. Frost top and sides of remaining cake. Place cake in the center of a large round tray (about 18 in.). Arrange chocolate chips on top of cake. Place sponge cakes around cake. Mix reserved frosting with milk; drizzle over sponge cakes. **Yield:** 22 servings.

Pumpkin Cake
with Caramel Sauce

If a recipe has pumpkin in it, it's likely I'll enjoy it! This one resulted when I added my favorite key ingredient to an old recipe for spice cake that I had.
—Roberta Peck, Fort Hill, Pennsylvania

2 cups all-purpose flour
2 cups sugar
2 teaspoons baking soda
2 teaspoons ground cinnamon
1 teaspoon ground nutmeg
1/2 teaspoon salt
4 eggs
1 can (16 ounces) solid-pack pumpkin
1 cup vegetable oil
CARAMEL SAUCE:
1-1/2 cups packed brown sugar
3 tablespoons all-purpose flour
Pinch salt
1-1/4 cups water
2 tablespoons butter
1/2 teaspoon vanilla extract

In a mixing bowl, combine the first six ingredients. In another bowl, beat eggs, pumpkin and oil until smooth; add to the dry ingredients. Mix until well blended, about 1 minute. Pour into a greased 13-in. x 9-in. x 2-in. baking pan. Bake at 350° for 35-40 minutes or until a toothpick inserted near the center comes out clean. Cool on a wire rack.

For sauce, combine brown sugar, flour and salt in a saucepan. Stir in water and butter; bring to a boil over medium heat. Boil for 3 minutes, stirring constantly. Remove from the heat; stir in vanilla. Cut cake into squares and serve with warm sauce. **Yield:** 12-15 servings.

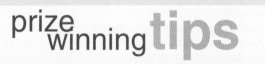

* * * *

With my from-scratch recipe for angel food cake, I often add part of a package of my favorite Jell-O flavor to the flour before it goes into the egg whites. It lends nice flavor and a pretty color.

—Mrs. Mervin Eash, Burr Oak, Michigan

What could be easier? I bake my lemon pound cake ahead and freeze it for last-minute get-togethers and family gatherings. To serve, I just thaw it and top with fresh fruit, ice cream or a dessert sauce.

—Barbara Wellons, Charlotte, Tennessee

Caramel Apple Cake

A wonderful harvest of apples that we picked up at a local orchard one year inspired me to adjust a recipe I'd seen and come up with this moist cake.
—Paulette Reyenga, Brantford, Ontario

- 1/2 cup chopped walnuts
- 1/3 cup packed brown sugar
- 1 cup flaked coconut
- 2-1/2 cups all-purpose flour
- 1-1/2 cups sugar
- 1-1/2 teaspoons baking soda
- 1 teaspoon salt
- 1/2 teaspoon baking powder
- 1/4 teaspoon ground cinnamon
- 2 eggs
- 1/2 cup evaporated milk
- 1/3 cup water
- 2 cups finely shredded peeled apples

CARAMEL TOPPING:
- 1/3 cup packed brown sugar
- 1/4 cup evaporated milk
- 2 tablespoons butter

Combine walnuts, brown sugar and coconut; set aside. In a mixing bowl, combine the next six ingredients. In a small bowl, combine eggs, milk, water and apples; add to flour mixture. Mix well. Pour into a greased 13-in. x 9-in. x 2-in. baking pan. Sprinkle with nut mixture. Bake at 325° for 45-50 minutes or until a toothpick inserted near the center comes out clean.

Meanwhile, in a heavy saucepan, combine the topping ingredients; cook over medium heat, stirring constantly, until the sugar is dissolved and the mixture has thickened slightly, about 8 minutes. Poke holes with a fork in top of the hot cake; immediately spoon topping over cake. Cool completely on a wire rack. **Yield:** 12-15 servings.

Buttermilk Banana Cake

When I was a girl, this was my family's favorite Sunday cake. Since I'm "nuts" about nuts, I added the pecans. —Arlene Grenz, Linton, North Dakota

- 3/4 cup butter, softened
- 1 cup sugar
- 1/2 cup packed brown sugar
- 2 eggs
- 1 cup mashed ripe banana
- 1 teaspoon vanilla extract
- 2 cups cake flour
- 1 teaspoon each baking powder and soda
- 1/2 teaspoon salt
- 1/2 cup buttermilk

FILLING/FROSTING:
- 1/2 cup half-and-half cream
- 1/2 cup sugar
- 2 tablespoons butter
- 2 tablespoons all-purpose flour
- 1/4 teaspoon salt
- 1 teaspoon vanilla extract
- 1/2 cup chopped pecans
- 2 cups heavy whipping cream
- 1/4 cup confectioners' sugar

In a mixing bowl, cream butter and sugars until fluffy. Add eggs; beat for 2 minutes. Add banana and vanilla; beat for 2 minutes. Combine the flour, baking powder, baking soda and salt; add to creamed mixture alternately with buttermilk. Pour into two greased and floured 9-in. round baking pans. Bake at 375° for 25-30 minutes or until a toothpick inserted near the center comes out clean. Cool in pans 10 minutes; remove to wire racks and cool completely.

For filling, combine half-and-half, sugar, butter, flour and salt in a saucepan. Bring to a boil; cook and stir for 2 minutes. Remove from the heat; stir in vanilla and pecans. Cool. Spread between cake layers.

For frosting, beat whipping cream until soft peaks form. Gradually beat in the confectioners' sugar; beat until stiff peaks form. Spread over top and sides of cake. Store in the refrigerator. **Yield:** 12-16 servings.

Cheesecakes

Deluxe Chip Cheesecake, p. 46

Neapolitan Cheesecake

(Pictured below)

This rich, creamy cheesecake is a crowd-pleasing standout. It has won first-place ribbons at numerous fairs and is my family's favorite dessert. It's an indulgence sure to produce oohs and aahs when served to guests. —Sherri Regalbuto
Carp, Ontario

    1 cup chocolate wafer crumbs
    5 tablespoons butter, melted, *divided*
    3 packages (8 ounces *each*) cream cheese, softened
3/4 cup sugar
    3 eggs
    1 teaspoon vanilla extract
    5 squares (1 ounce *each*) semisweet chocolate, *divided*
2-1/2 squares (2-1/2 ounces) white baking chocolate, *divided*
    1/3 cup mashed sweetened strawberries
    2 teaspoons shortening, *divided*

Combine crumbs and 3 tablespoons of butter; press onto the bottom of an ungreased 9-in. springform pan. Place pan on a baking sheet. Bake at 350° for 8 minutes; cool.

In a mixing bowl, beat the cream cheese and sugar until smooth. Beat in eggs, one at a time, beating well after each addition. Add vanilla. Divide into three portions, about 1-2/3 cups each. Melt 2 squares semisweet chocolate; stir into one portion of batter. Melt 2 squares of white chocolate; stir into second portion. Stir strawberries into remaining batter. Spread semisweet mixture evenly over crust. Carefully spread with white chocolate mixture, then strawberry mixture.

Place pan on a baking sheet. Bake at 425° for 10 minutes; reduce heat to 300°. Bake 50-55 minutes or until center is nearly set. Remove from oven; immediately run a knife around edge. Cool; remove from pan.

Melt remaining semisweet chocolate, remaining butter and 1 teaspoon of shortening; cool for 2 minutes. Pour over cake.

Melt remaining white chocolate and shortening; drizzle over glaze. Refrigerate leftovers. **Yield:** 12-14 servings.

Banana Cream Cheesecake

If you like the flavor of banana cream pie, you'll absolutely love this cheesecake! This lovely company-worthy dessert can be made a day or two in advance before serving. —Margie Snodgrass
Wilmore, Kentucky

1-3/4 cups graham cracker crumbs (about 28 squares)
    1/4 cup sugar
    1/2 cup butter, melted
    1 package (8 ounces) cream cheese, softened
    1/2 cup sugar
    1 carton (8 ounces) frozen whipped topping, thawed, *divided*
    3 to 4 medium firm bananas, sliced
1-3/4 cups cold milk
    1 package (3.4 ounces) instant banana cream pudding mix

In a small bowl, combine the graham cracker crumbs and sugar; stir in the butter. Set aside 1/2 cup for topping. Press remaining crumb mixture onto the bottom and up the sides of a greased 9-in. springform pan or 9-in. square baking pan. Place pan on a baking sheet. Bake at 350° for 5-7 minutes. Cool on a wire rack.

In a mixing bowl, beat the cream cheese and sugar until smooth. Fold in 2 cups of the whipped topping. Arrange half of the banana slices in the crust; top with half of the cream cheese mixture. Repeat layers.

In a bowl, beat milk and pudding mix until smooth; fold in remaining whipped topping. Pour over the cream cheese layer. Sprinkle with reserved crumb mixture. Refrigerate for 1-2 hours or until set. **Yield:** 10 servings.

Apple Cheesecake

After a big meal, this fluffy no-bake cheesecake with its deliciously different applesauce and peanut topping really hits the spot. It needs no crust, and the light cheese layer is smooth and creamy.
                                    —Adeline Piscitelli,
                                    Sayreville, New Jersey

    2 envelopes unflavored gelatin
1/3 cup cold water
1-3/4 cups apple juice
1/2 cup sugar
    3 egg yolks, beaten
    3 packages (8 ounces *each*) cream
        cheese, softened
1/2 teaspoon ground cinnamon
1/4 teaspoon ground nutmeg
    1 cup heavy whipping cream, whipped
TOPPING:
1/2 cup chopped dry roasted peanuts
    2 tablespoons butter

1 cup applesauce
1/3 cup packed brown sugar
1/4 teaspoon ground cinnamon
**Additional whipped cream, cinnamon and
    peanuts, optional**

In a small bowl, soften gelatin in water; let stand for 2 minutes. In a saucepan over medium heat, cook and stir apple juice, sugar, egg yolks and gelatin mixture until gelatin is dissolved. Cool to room temperature.

In a large mixing bowl, beat the cream cheese, cinnamon and nutmeg until smooth. Gradually beat in gelatin mixture until smooth. Chill until slightly thickened, about 20 minutes. Fold in cream. Pour into an ungreased 9-in. springform pan. Chill 4 hours or overnight.

In a saucepan over medium heat, brown the peanuts in butter for 2 minutes. Add applesauce, brown sugar and cinnamon; cook and stir for 5 minutes. Cool. Spread over top of cheesecake. If desired, garnish with whipped cream, cinnamon and peanuts. **Yield:** 12-16 servings.

dough onto the bottom and up the sides of each cup. In a mixing bowl, beat cream cheese and sugar until smooth. Beat in milk and vanilla. Add egg; beat on low just until combined. Spoon about 1 tablespoonful into each cup.

Bake at 325° for 15-18 minutes or until set. Cool on a wire rack for 30 minutes. Carefully remove from pans to cool completely. Top with pie filling. Store in the refrigerator. **Yield:** 2 dozen.

Deluxe Chip Cheesecake

(Pictured on page 43)

My husband and I love cheesecake. Once, when we were asked to make a dessert for a "traveling basket" for our church, we prepared this luscious layered treat. It looked so good, we couldn't bear to give it away. We ended up contributing another sweet treat instead!
—Kari Gollup
Madison, Wisconsin

1-1/2 cups vanilla wafer crumbs
  1/2 cup confectioners' sugar
  1/4 cup baking cocoa
  1/3 cup butter, melted
FILLING:
  3 packages (8 ounces *each*) cream cheese, softened
  3/4 cup sugar
  1/3 cup sour cream
  3 tablespoons all-purpose flour
  1 teaspoon vanilla extract
  1/4 teaspoon salt
  3 eggs
  1 cup butterscotch chips, melted
  1 cup semisweet chocolate chips, melted
  1 cup vanilla *or* white chips, melted
TOPPING:
  1 tablespoon *each* butterscotch, semisweet and vanilla *or* white chips
1-1/2 teaspoons shortening

In a bowl, combine wafer crumbs, confectioners' sugar, cocoa and butter. Press onto the bottom and 1-1/2 in. up the sides of a greased 9-in. springform pan. Place pan on a baking sheet. Bake at 350° for 7-9 minutes or until set. Cool on a wire rack.

In a mixing bowl, beat cream cheese and sugar until smooth. Add sour cream, flour, vanilla and salt; mix well. Add eggs; beat on low speed just until combined. Remove 1-1/2 cups batter to a bowl; stir in butterscotch chips. Pour over crust. Add chocolate chips to another 1-1/2 cups batter; carefully spoon over butterscotch layer. Stir vanilla chips into remaining batter; spoon over chocolate layer.

Place pan on a baking sheet. Bake at 350° for 55-60 minutes or until center is almost set. Cool

Tiny Cherry Cheesecakes

(Pictured above)

I prepare these mini cheesecakes every Christmas and for many weddings. I've received countless compliments and recipe requests. When I send these along in my husband's lunch, I have to be sure to pack extras because the men he works with love them, too.
—Janice Hertlein
Esterhazy, Saskatchewan

  1 cup all-purpose flour
  1/3 cup sugar
  1/4 cup baking cocoa
  1/2 cup cold butter
  2 tablespoons cold water
FILLING:
  2 packages (3 ounces *each*) cream cheese, softened
  1/4 cup sugar
  2 tablespoons milk
  1 teaspoon vanilla extract
  1 egg
  1 can (21 ounces) cherry *or* strawberry pie filling

In a small bowl, combine flour, sugar and cocoa; cut in butter until crumbly. Gradually add water, tossing with a fork until dough forms a ball. Shape into 24 balls. Place in greased miniature muffin cups; press

on a wire rack for 10 minutes. Carefully run a knife around edge of pan to loosen. Cool for 1 hour.

For topping, place each flavor of chips and 1/2 teaspoon shortening in three small microwave-safe bowls. Microwave on high for 25 seconds; stir. Heat in 10- to 20-second intervals, stirring until smooth. Drizzle over cheesecake. Chill for at least 3 hours. Remove sides of pan. Refrigerate leftovers. **Yield:** 12-14 servings.

Nutty Cheesecake Squares

I grew up on a farm and have had a lot of good recipes handed down to me. This is one of my favorite desserts to serve when guests come over or at family gatherings and church suppers.
—Ruth Simon, Buffalo, New York

  2 cups all-purpose flour
  1 cup finely chopped walnuts
  2/3 cup packed brown sugar
  1/2 teaspoon salt
  2/3 cup butter
FILLING:
  2 packages (8 ounces *each*) cream
    cheese, softened
  1/2 cup sugar
  2 eggs
  1/4 cup milk
  1 teaspoon vanilla extract

In a bowl, combine flour, walnuts, brown sugar and salt; cut in butter until the mixture resembles coarse crumbs. Set half aside; press remaining crumb mixture onto the bottom of a greased 13-in. x 9-in. x 2-in. baking pan. Bake at 350° for 10-15 minutes or until lightly browned.

In a mixing bowl, beat filling ingredients until smooth; pour over crust. Sprinkle with reserved crumb mixture. Bake at 350° for 20-25 minutes or until a knife inserted near the center comes out clean. Cool completely. Store in the refrigerator. **Yield:** 16-20 servings.

Orange Chip Cheesecake

(Pictured at right)

I love to adapt and mix recipes, which led to the creation of this creamy treat many years ago. It came to mind immediately when I was planning an orange theme menu for a party. In this case, the distinctive citrus flavor is complemented by chocolate!
—Susan West, North Grafton, Massachusetts

 12 ounces cream cheese, softened
1/2 cup sugar
  2 eggs
1/2 teaspoon salt
1/2 teaspoon orange extract
3/4 to 1 cup miniature semisweet chocolate
    chips
  1 chocolate crumb *or* graham cracker
    crust (9 inches)
TOPPING:
1-1/2 cups (12 ounces) sour cream
  2 tablespoons sugar
1/2 teaspoon vanilla extract
  1 can (11 ounces) mandarin oranges,
    drained
Additional chocolate chips

In a mixing bowl, beat cream cheese and sugar until smooth. Add eggs; beat on low speed just until combined. Add salt and orange extract; beat just until blended. Stir in chocolate chips. Pour into crust. Bake at 375° for 20 minutes or until center is almost set. Remove from the oven; increase temperature to 425°.

In a bowl, combine sour cream, sugar and vanilla; spread over cheesecake. Bake 5 minutes longer. Cool on a wire rack for 15 minutes. Refrigerate overnight. Just before serving, garnish with oranges and additional chocolate chips. **Yield:** 8 servings.

Luscious Almond Cheesecake

(Pictured below)

I received this recipe along with a set of spring-form pans from a cousin at my wedding shower many years ago. It makes a heavenly cheesecake that my son Tommy often requests for his birthday instead of the more traditional layer cake.
—Brenda Clifford, Overland Park, Kansas

CRUST:
1-1/4 cups crushed vanilla wafers
3/4 cup finely chopped almonds
1/4 cup sugar
1/3 cup butter, melted
FILLING:
4 packages (8 ounces *each*) cream
  cheese, softened
1-1/4 cups sugar
4 eggs
1-1/2 teaspoons almond extract
1 teaspoon vanilla extract
TOPPING:
2 cups (16 ounces) sour cream
1/4 cup sugar
1 teaspoon vanilla extract
1/8 cup toasted sliced almonds

In a bowl, combine the crushed vanilla wafers, almonds and sugar; add the butter and mix well. Press into the bottom of an ungreased 10-in. springform pan; set aside.

In a large mixing bowl, beat cream cheese and sugar until creamy. Add eggs, one at a time, beating well after each addition. Add extracts; beat just until blended. Pour into crust. Place pan on a baking sheet. Bake at 350° for 55 minutes or until center is almost set.

Remove from the oven; let stand for 5 minutes. Combine sour cream, sugar and vanilla; spread over filling. Return to the oven for 5 minutes. Cool on a wire rack for 10 minutes. Run a knife around edge of pan to loosen; cool completely. Chill overnight.

Just before serving, sprinkle with almonds and remove sides of pan. Store in the refrigerator. **Yield:** 14-16 servings.

Caramel Fudge Cheesecake

It's hard to resist this chocolaty cheesecake with its fudgy crust, crunchy pecans and gooey layer of caramel. I combined several recipes to create this version, which satisfies both the chocolate lovers and the cheesecake lovers in my family.
—Brenda Ruse, Truro, Nova Scotia

1 package fudge brownie mix (8-inch
  square pan size)
1 package (14 ounces) caramels
1/4 cup evaporated milk
1-1/4 cups coarsely chopped pecans
2 packages (8 ounces *each*) cream
  cheese, softened
1/2 cup sugar
2 eggs
2 squares (1 ounce *each*) semisweet
  chocolate, melted
2 squares (1 ounce *each*) unsweetened
  chocolate, melted

Prepare the brownie batter according to the package directions. Spread batter into a greased 9-in. springform pan. Place pan on a baking sheet. Bake at 350° for 20 minutes. Cool for 10 minutes on a wire rack.

Meanwhile, in a microwave-safe bowl, melt caramels with milk. Pour over brownie crust; sprinkle with pecans. In a mixing bowl, combine the cream cheese and sugar; mix well. Add eggs, beating on low speed just until combined. Stir in melted chocolate. Pour over pecans.

Place pan on a baking sheet. Bake at 350° for 35-40 minutes or until the center is almost set. Cool on a wire rack for 10 minutes. Run a knife around edge of pan to loosen; cool completely. Chill overnight. Remove sides of pan before serving. Store any leftovers in the refrigerator. **Yield:** 12 servings.

Editor's Note: This recipe was tested with Hershey caramels.

Family-Favorite Cheesecake

This fluffy, delicate cheesecake has been a family favorite for over 20 years. I've shared it at many gatherings over the years.   —Esther Wappner
Mansfield, Ohio

**2-1/2 cups graham cracker crumbs (about 40
    squares)**
1/3 cup sugar
1/2 teaspoon ground cinnamon
1/2 cup butter, melted
FILLING:
**3 packages (8 ounces *each*) cream
    cheese, softened**
1-1/2 cups sugar
1 teaspoon vanilla extract
4 eggs, *separated*
TOPPING:
1/2 cup sour cream
2 tablespoons sugar
1/2 teaspoon vanilla extract
1/2 cup heavy whipping cream, whipped

In a small bowl, combine the cracker crumbs, sugar and cinnamon; stir in butter. Press onto the bottom and 2 in. up the sides of a greased 9-in. springform pan. Place pan on a baking sheet. Bake at 350° for 5 minutes. Cool on a wire rack. Reduce heat to 325°.

In a mixing bowl, beat cream cheese, sugar and vanilla until smooth. Add egg yolks; beat on low just until combined. In a small mixing bowl, beat egg whites until soft peaks form; fold into cream cheese mixture. Pour over crust.

Place pan on a baking sheet. Bake for 1 hour or until center is almost set. Cool on a wire rack for 10 minutes. Carefully run a knife around edge of pan to loosen; cool 1 hour longer. Refrigerate until completely cooled.

Combine the sour cream, sugar and vanilla; fold in whipped cream. Spread over cheesecake. Refrigerate overnight. Remove sides of pan. **Yield:** 12 servings.

Crustless New York Cheesecake

(Pictured above right)

This rich and flavorful cheesecake uses an abundance of dairy products. Even though the cake doesn't have a crust, everyone loves it.
   —Mrs. George Parsell, Flushing, New York

1-1/2 cups sugar
3 tablespoons cornstarch
3 cups (24 ounces) ricotta cheese
2 tablespoons lemon juice
**2 packages (8 ounces *each*) cream
    cheese, softened**
1/2 cup butter, softened
4 eggs
1 teaspoon vanilla extract
2 cups (16 ounces) sour cream
3 tablespoons all-purpose flour
Assorted fresh fruit

In a large mixing bowl, combine the sugar, cornstarch, ricotta and lemon juice until smooth. Add cream cheese and butter; mix well. Add eggs and vanilla; beat on low speed just until combined. Add sour cream and flour; beat just until combined. Pour into a greased 9-in. springform pan. Place pan on a baking sheet.

Bake at 325° for 70-75 minutes or until edges are lightly browned and top is dry to the touch (center 5 in. of cheesecake will not be set). Cool on a wire rack for 10 minutes. Carefully run a knife around the edge of pan to loosen; cool 1 hour longer. Refrigerate overnight. Remove sides of pan. Garnish with fruit. Refrigerate leftovers. **Yield:** 12-16 servings.

The Skinny on Cream Cheese

For the best results, don't use reduced-fat or fat-free cream cheese to make cheesecakes. Always soften cream cheese at room temperature before mixing.

Black 'n' White Cheesecake Bars

(Pictured above)

Whenever it's my turn to make dessert for our local fire department auxiliary meeting, I always get requests to bring this delicious recipe.
—Bertille Cooper, St. Inigoes, Maryland

> 2 cups (12 ounces) semisweet chocolate chips
> 1/2 cup butter
> 2 cups graham cracker crumbs
> 1 package (8 ounces) cream cheese, softened
> 1 can (14 ounces) sweetened condensed milk
> 1 egg
> 1 teaspoon vanilla extract

In a double boiler or microwave, melt chocolate chips and butter, stirring occasionally. Stir in the graham cracker crumbs. Set aside 1/4 cup for topping. Press the remaining crumbs into an ungreased 13-in. x 9-in. x 2-in. baking pan.

In a mixing bowl, beat cream cheese until smooth. Gradually beat in milk, egg and vanilla. Pour over the crust. Sprinkle with the reserved crumbs. Bake at 325° for 25-30 minutes or until lightly browned. Cool. Refrigerate for 3 hours or until completely chilled. Cut into bars. Store in the refrigerator. **Yield:** 4 dozen.

Editor's Note: Bars may be frozen for up to 3 months.

Chocolate Cheesecake

Everyone's a chocolate lover when it comes to this special dessert. "It melts in your mouth!" and "Very smooth and fudgy!" are typical comments I've heard after guests take a bite. For a fun taste twist, spoon cherry or strawberry topping over each slice. —Sue Call, Beech Grove, Indiana

> 1 cup crushed chocolate wafer crumbs
> 3 tablespoons sugar
> 3 tablespoons butter, melted
> FILLING:
> 2 cups (12 ounces) semisweet chocolate chips
> 2 packages (8 ounces *each*) cream cheese, softened
> 3/4 cup sugar
> 2 tablespoons all-purpose flour
> 2 eggs
> 1 teaspoon vanilla extract
> Strawberries and white chocolate shavings, optional

In a small bowl, combine cookie crumbs and sugar; stir in butter. Press onto the bottom of a greased 9-in. springform pan; set aside. In a saucepan over low heat, melt the chocolate chips; stir until smooth. Set aside.

In a mixing bowl, beat cream cheese and sugar until smooth. Add flour and beat well. Add eggs; beat on low just until combined. Stir in vanilla and melted chocolate just until blended. Pour over crust.

Place pan on a baking sheet. Bake at 350° for 40-45 minutes or until center is almost set. Cool on a wire rack for 10 minutes. Carefully run a knife around edge of pan to loosen; cool 1 hour longer. Chill overnight.

Remove sides of pan. Garnish slices with strawberries and chocolate shavings if desired. Refrigerate leftovers. **Yield:** 12 servings.

Cheesecake Done?

A cheesecake is done when the edges are slightly puffed and the center (about the size of a walnut) is still soft and moist. The center will firm upon cooling. A crack in the cheesecake may be an indicator of overbaking.

You can cover cracks with a topping such as sour cream, whipped cream or your favorite fresh berries.

Pumpkin Cheesecake with Sour Cream Topping

Why not surprise Thanksgiving guests with this luscious cheesecake instead of the traditional pie?
—Dorothy Smith, El Dorado, Arkansas

1-1/2 cups graham cracker crumbs
  1/4 cup sugar
  1/3 cup butter, melted
FILLING:
    3 packages (8 ounces *each*) cream cheese, softened
    1 cup packed brown sugar
    1 can (15 ounces) solid-pack pumpkin
    2 tablespoons cornstarch
1-1/4 teaspoons ground cinnamon
  1/2 teaspoon ground nutmeg
    1 can (5 ounces) evaporated milk
    2 eggs
TOPPING:
    2 cups (16 ounces) sour cream
  1/3 cup sugar
    1 teaspoon vanilla extract
Additional ground cinnamon

In a bowl, combine crumbs and sugar; stir in butter. Press onto the bottom and 1-1/2 in. up the sides of a greased 9-in. springform pan. Place pan on a baking sheet. Bake at 350° for 5-7 minutes or until set. Cool for 10 minutes.

In a mixing bowl, beat cream cheese and brown sugar until smooth. Add the pumpkin, cornstarch, cinnamon and nutmeg; mix well. Gradually beat in milk and eggs just until blended. Pour into crust.

Place pan on a baking sheet. Bake at 350° for 55-60 minutes or until center is almost set. Combine the sour cream, sugar and vanilla; spread over filling. Bake 5 minutes longer. Cool on a wire rack for 10 minutes. Carefully run a knife around edge of pan to loosen; cool 1 hour longer. Chill overnight.

Remove sides of pan; let stand at room temperature 30 minutes before slicing. Sprinkle with cinnamon. Refrigerate leftovers. **Yield:** 12-14 servings.

Tangy Lemon Cheesecake

(Pictured at right)

This dessert gets added spark from a gingersnap crust and a luscious lemon sauce. The mix of sweet and tart is unexpected and delightful. I came up with the recipe based on several others.
—Pam Persons, Towanda, Kansas

2-1/2 cups crushed gingersnaps (about 40 cookies)
  1/3 cup butter, melted

FILLING:
    3 packages (8 ounces *each*) cream cheese, softened
    1 cup sugar
    3 eggs
    1 tablespoon lemon juice
    1 tablespoon vanilla extract
SAUCE:
  1/2 cup sugar
    2 tablespoons cornstarch
  3/4 cup water
    2 tablespoons butter
  1/4 cup lemon juice
    1 tablespoon grated lemon peel

In a small bowl, combine cookie crumbs and butter; mix well. Press onto the bottom and 2 in. up the sides of a greased 9-in. springform pan; set aside.

In a mixing bowl, beat cream cheese and sugar until smooth. Add eggs; beat on low just until combined. Add lemon juice and vanilla; beat just until blended. Pour into crust.

Place pan on a baking sheet. Bake at 350° for 35-40 minutes or until center is almost set. Cool on a wire rack for 10 minutes. Carefully run a knife around the edge of pan to loosen; cool 1 hour longer.

In a saucepan, combine sugar and cornstarch. Stir in water until smooth; bring to a boil. Reduce heat; cook and stir over medium heat for 2 minutes or until thickened. Remove from the heat; stir in butter, lemon juice and peel. Refrigerate cheesecake and sauce overnight. Serve the sauce over cheesecake. **Yield:** 12 servings.

Cool Lime Cheesecake

I started baking this treat several years ago, and it immediately won raves. The mixture of tart lime and sweet creamy cheesecake is absolutely scrumptious. At any get-together, it is a showstopping dessert that's always enjoyed. —Karen Donhauser
Frazer, Pennsylvania

2-1/4 cups graham cracker crumbs (about 36
    squares)
  1/3 cup sugar
  1/2 cup butter, melted
FILLING:
  20 ounces cream cheese, softened
  3/4 cup sugar
    1 cup (8 ounces) sour cream
    3 tablespoons all-purpose flour
    3 eggs
  2/3 cup lime juice
    1 teaspoon vanilla extract
    1 drop green food coloring, optional
Whipped cream and lime slices

In a bowl, combine the graham cracker crumbs and sugar; stir in the butter. Press onto the bottom and 1 in. up the side of a greased 10-in. springform pan. Place pan on a baking sheet. Bake at 375° for 8 minutes. Cool.

In a mixing bowl, beat cream cheese and sugar until smooth. Add sour cream and flour; beat well. Beat in eggs on low speed just until combined. Stir in lime juice, vanilla and food coloring if desired just until mixed. Pour into crust.

Place pan on a baking sheet. Bake at 325° for 50-55 minutes or until center is almost set. Cool on a wire rack for 1 hour. Refrigerate overnight. Remove sides of pan. Garnish with whipped cream and lime. **Yield:** 12-14 servings.

Mini Apricot Cheesecakes

I rely on vanilla wafers to create the no-fuss crusts for these darling individual cheesecake desserts. For a different look and taste, vary the kind of preserves that tops these tempting treats. I guarantee that guests are sure to help themselves to "just one more." —Carol Twardzik
Spy Hill, Saskatchewan

  24 vanilla wafers
    2 packages (8 ounces *each*) cream
      cheese, softened
  3/4 cup sugar
    2 eggs
    1 tablespoon lemon juice
    1 teaspoon vanilla extract
    1 cup apricot preserves

Place wafers flat side down in paper- or foil-lined muffin cups; set aside. In a mixing bowl, beat cream cheese and sugar until smooth. Add the eggs, lemon juice and vanilla; beat well. Fill muffin cups three-fourths full. Place on a baking sheet.

Bake at 375° for 17-20 minutes or until top is set. Cool on a wire rack for 20 minutes. Top each cheesecake with 2 teaspoons preserves. Refrigerate until serving. **Yield:** 2 dozen.

Peanut Butter Cheesecake

The first time I served this cheesecake, my friends all went wild over it. They were surprised when I told them the crust is made of pretzels. The pairing of sweet and salty, and creamy and crunchy— plus peanut butter and chocolate—left everyone asking for another slice. —Lois Brooks
Newark, Delaware

1-1/2 cups crushed pretzels
  1/3 cup butter, melted
FILLING:
    5 packages (8 ounces *each*) cream
      cheese, softened
1-1/2 cups sugar
  3/4 cup creamy peanut butter
    2 teaspoons vanilla extract
    3 eggs
    1 cup peanut butter chips
    1 cup semisweet chocolate chips
TOPPING:
    1 cup (8 ounces) sour cream
    3 tablespoons creamy peanut butter
  1/2 cup sugar
  1/2 cup finely chopped unsalted
    peanuts

In a small bowl, combine the crushed pretzels and butter. Press onto the bottom and 1 in. up the sides of a greased 10-in. springform pan. Place pan on a baking sheet. Bake at 350° for 5 minutes. Cool on a wire rack.

In a mixing bowl, beat cream cheese and sugar until smooth. Add peanut butter and vanilla; mix well. Add eggs; beat on low just until combined. Stir in chips. Pour over the crust.

Place pan on a baking sheet. Bake at 350° for 50-55 minutes or until center is almost set. Cool on a wire rack for 15 minutes (leave the oven on).

Meanwhile, in a mixing bowl, combine sour cream, peanut butter and sugar; spread over filling. Sprinkle with nuts. Return to the oven for 5 minutes. Cool on a wire rack for 10 minutes. Carefully run a knife around the edge of the pan to loosen; cool 1 hour longer. Refrigerate overnight. Remove sides of pan. **Yield:** 12-14 servings.

Trifles

Chocolate and Fruit Trifle, p. 54

Cappuccino Mousse Trifle

(Pictured below)

This is the easiest trifle I've ever made, yet it looks like I spent so much time on it. I like to pipe whipped topping around the edge of the bowl, grate chocolate in the center and sprinkle with cinnamon. It gets rave reviews. —Tracy Bergland
Prior Lake, Minnesota

2-1/2 cups cold milk
   1/3 cup instant coffee granules
    2 packages (3.4 ounces *each*) instant vanilla pudding mix
    1 carton (16 ounces) frozen whipped topping, thawed, *divided*
    2 loaves (10-3/4 ounces *each*) frozen pound cake, thawed and cubed
    1 square (1 ounce) semisweet chocolate, grated
   1/4 teaspoon ground cinnamon

In a mixing bowl, stir the milk and coffee granules until dissolved; remove 1 cup and set aside. Add pudding mixes to the remaining milk mixture; beat on low speed for 2 minutes or until thickened. Fold in half of the whipped topping.

Place a third of the cake cubes in a 4-qt. serving or trifle bowl; layer with a third of the reserved milk mixture and pudding mixture and a fourth of the grated chocolate. Repeat layers twice. Garnish with remaining whipped topping and chocolate. Sprinkle with cinnamon. Cover and refrigerate until serving. **Yield: 16-20 servings.**

Blueberry Lemon Trifle

A refreshing lemon filling and fresh blueberries give this sunny dessert sensation plenty of color. Don't worry about heating up the oven. This doesn't require baking. —Ellen Peden, Houston, Texas

    3 cups fresh blueberries, *divided*
    2 cans (15-3/4 ounces *each*) lemon pie filling
    2 cartons (8 ounces *each*) lemon yogurt
    1 prepared angel food cake (8 inches), cut into 1-inch cubes
    1 carton (8 ounces) frozen whipped topping, thawed
Lemon slices and fresh mint, optional

Set aside 1/4 cup blueberries for garnish. In a bowl, combine pie filling and yogurt. In a 3-1/2-qt. serving or trifle bowl, layer a third of the cake cubes, lemon mixture and blueberries. Repeat layers twice. Top with whipped topping.

Cover and refrigerate for at least 2 hours. Garnish with reserved blueberries, and lemon and mint if desired. **Yield: 12-14 servings.**

Chocolate and Fruit Trifle

(Pictured on page 53)

This beautiful dessert layered with devil's food cake, a creamy pudding mixture, red berries and green kiwi is perfect for the holidays.
—Angie Dierikx, State Center, Iowa

    1 package (18-1/4 ounces) devil's food cake mix
    1 can (14 ounces) sweetened condensed milk
    1 cup cold water
    1 package (3.4 ounces) instant vanilla pudding mix
    2 cups heavy whipping cream, whipped
    2 tablespoons orange juice
    2 cups fresh strawberries, chopped
    2 cups fresh raspberries
    2 kiwifruit, peeled and chopped

Prepare cake batter according to package directions; pour into a greased 15-in. x 10-in. x 1-in. baking pan. Bake at 350° for 20 minutes or until a toothpick inserted near the center comes out clean. Cool completely on a wire rack. Crumble enough cake to measure 8 cups; set aside. (Save remaining cake for another use.)

In a mixing bowl, combine milk and water until smooth. Add pudding mix; beat on low speed for

2 minutes or until slightly thickened. Fold in the whipped cream.

To assemble, spread 2-1/2 cups pudding mixture in a 4-qt. glass bowl. Top with half of the crumbled cake; sprinkle with 1 tablespoon orange juice. Arrange half of the berries and kiwi over cake. Repeat pudding and cake layers; sprinkle with remaining orange juice. Top with remaining pudding mixture. Spoon remaining fruit around edge of bowl. Cover and refrigerate until serving. **Yield:** 12-16 servings.

Fruity Angel Food Trifle

This summery dessert showcases an attractive assortment of fresh and canned fruit. I refined the original recipe over time to suit our family's tastes.
—*Louise Bouvier, Lafleche, Saskatchewan*

- **4 cups cold milk**
- **2 packages (3.4 ounces *each*) instant vanilla pudding mix**
- **1 prepared angel food cake (8 inches)**
- **1 carton (8 ounces) frozen whipped topping, thawed**
- **1 can (20 ounces) pineapple tidbits, drained**
- **1 can (15 ounces) sliced pears, drained**
- **1 pint strawberries, sliced**
- **4 kiwifruit, peeled, halved and thinly sliced**
- **1 cup fresh *or* frozen blueberries, thawed**

In a mixing bowl, beat milk and pudding mix on low speed for 2 minutes; set aside. Split cake horizontally into thirds; place one layer in a 5-qt. serving bowl that is 9 in. in diameter. Top with a third of the pudding, whipped topping and fruit. Repeat layers twice. Cover and chill for at least 3 hours. **Yield:** 16-20 servings.

Editor's Note: Before assembling trifle, check to make sure that the diameter of your serving bowl is large enough to accommodate the diameter of your cake. If the cake is too large, trim it to fit or cut into cubes.

Strawberry Banana Trifle

(Pictured above right)

No matter where I take this dessert, the bowl gets emptied in minutes. It's fun to make because everyone oohs and ahhs over how pretty it is.
—*Kim Waterhouse, Randolph, Maine*

- **1 cup sugar**
- **1/4 cup cornstarch**

- **3 tablespoons strawberry gelatin powder**
- **1 cup cold water**
- **1 pint fresh strawberries, sliced**
- **1-3/4 cups cold milk**
- **1 package (3.4 ounces) instant vanilla pudding mix**
- **3 medium firm bananas, sliced**
- **1 tablespoon lemon juice**
- **6 cups cubed angel food cake**
- **2 cups heavy whipping cream, whipped**
- **Additional strawberries *or* banana slices, optional**

In a saucepan, combine the sugar, cornstarch and gelatin; stir in water until smooth. Bring to a boil; cook and stir for 2 minutes or until thickened. Remove from the heat. Stir in strawberries; set aside. In a mixing bowl, combine milk and pudding mix. Beat on low speed for 2 minutes; set aside. Toss bananas with lemon juice; drain and set aside.

Place half of the cake cubes in a trifle bowl or 3-qt. serving bowl. Layer with half of the pudding, bananas, strawberry sauce and whipped cream. Repeat layers. Cover and refrigerate for at least 2 hours. Garnish with additional fruit if desired. **Yield:** 14 servings.

mixes on low speed for 2 minutes.

To assemble, crumble half of the cake into a 4-qt. trifle bowl or large bowl. Layer with half of the peanut butter sauce, pudding, whipped topping and candy bars; repeat layers. Cover and refrigerate for at least 3 hours before serving. **Yield:** 12-15 servings.

Banana Macaroon Trifle

A chewy homemade macaroon mixture takes the place traditionally held by cake in this trifle. Sometimes I serve the sweet treat in individual cups. No time to bake? Use store-bought macaroons.
—Barbara Keith, Faucett, Missouri

        2 tablespoons butter, softened
        1 cup sugar
        1 egg
        1 cup flaked coconut
    1/2 cup old-fashioned oats
        2 tablespoons all-purpose flour
        1 teaspoon baking powder
    1/4 cup milk
        1 teaspoon vanilla extract
        3 to 4 small firm bananas, sliced
        1 tablespoon pineapple juice
        1 carton (12 ounces) frozen whipped
            topping, thawed

For macaroon mixture, beat butter and sugar in a mixing bowl until well blended. Add egg; mix well. Combine coconut, oats, flour and baking powder. Combine milk and vanilla; add to the sugar mixture alternately with coconut mixture (mixture will appear curdled).

Spread in a well-greased 13-in. x 9-in. x 2-in. baking pan. Bake at 325° for 25-30 minutes or until edges are golden brown. Cool completely; crumble. Set aside 1/4 cup for topping.

Just before serving, toss bananas with pineapple juice. In a 2-1/2-qt. serving bowl, layer a third of the macaroon crumbs, whipped topping and bananas. Repeat layers twice. Sprinkle with reserved crumbs. **Yield:** 8-10 servings.

Sweetheart Trifle

(Pictured above)

If you're a peanut butter and chocolate lover, this fantastic trifle is for you. It's a hit every time I serve it. I always have requests for the recipe.
—Lorie Cooper, Chatham, Ontario

        1 package (18-1/4 ounces) chocolate cake
            mix
        1 package (10 ounces) peanut butter
            chips
    4-1/4 cups cold milk, *divided*
    1/2 cup heavy whipping cream
    1/4 teaspoon vanilla extract
        2 packages (5.9 ounces *each*) instant
            chocolate pudding mix
        1 carton (12 ounces) frozen whipped
            topping, thawed
        4 Nestle Crunch candy bars (1.55 ounces
            each), crumbled

Prepare cake mix according to package directions. Pour the batter into a greased 13-in. x 9-in. x 2-in. baking pan. Bake at 350° for 30-35 minutes or until a toothpick inserted near the center comes out clean. Cool on a wire rack.

In a heavy saucepan, combine chips, 1/4 cup milk and cream. Cook and stir over low heat until chips are melted. Remove from the heat; stir in vanilla. Cool to room temperature. Place the remaining milk in a mixing bowl; beat in pudding

Apple Spice Cake Trifle

We like this trifle because it's economical, looks elegant and tastes delicious. Our friends have enjoyed it and requested the recipe.
—Nora Lee Ingle, Swan, Iowa

        1 package (18-1/4 ounces) spice cake mix
    1-1/4 cups cinnamon applesauce
        3 eggs
    1/3 cup vegetable oil

- **1 can (21 ounces) apple pie filling**
- **1 tablespoon butter**
- **7 teaspoons ground cinnamon,** *divided*
- **3 cups cold milk**
- **1 package (5.1 ounces) instant vanilla pudding mix**
- **1 envelope whipped topping mix**
- **1 carton (12 ounces) frozen whipped topping, thawed**
- **1/2 cup chopped walnuts**
- **1/4 cup English toffee bits** *or* **almond brickle chips**

In a mixing bowl, combine dry cake mix, apple-sauce, eggs and oil; beat on medium speed for 2 minutes. Pour into a greased 13-in. x 9-in. x 2-in. baking pan. Bake at 350° for 35-40 minutes or until a toothpick inserted near the center comes out clean. Cool on a wire rack.

In a saucepan, cook pie filling, butter and 1 teaspoon cinnamon until butter is melted; stir until well blended. Cool. In a mixing bowl, combine milk, pudding mix, topping mix and remaining cinnamon. Beat on high until thickened, about 5 minutes. Let stand 5 minutes.

Spread a third of the topping in a 6-qt. bowl. Cut cake into cubes; place half over topping. Top with half of the fruit mixture, walnuts and pudding mixture. Repeat layers, ending with remaining topping mixture. Sprinkle with toffee bits. Cover and chill for at least 2 hours. **Yield:** 20-24 servings.

Coconut Chocolate Trifle

This luscious dessert will wow everyone who sees it, let alone tries it. Apricot preserves add a fruity touch to the pleasing pairing of chocolate and toasted coconut in this easy-to-assemble trifle.
—Donna Cline, Pensacola, Florida

- **1 loaf (10-3/4 ounces) frozen pound cake, thawed**
- **1/3 cup apricot preserves**
- **1/3 cup plus 2 tablespoons orange juice,** *divided*
- **1 package (4 ounces) German sweet chocolate**
- **1-1/4 cups flaked coconut, toasted,** *divided*
- **1-3/4 cups cold milk**
- **1 cup half-and-half cream**
- **1 package (5.9 ounces) instant chocolate pudding mix**

Trim crust from top, sides and bottom of cake. Cut cake into 16 slices. Spread preserves over eight slices; top with remaining cake. Cut into 1-in. cubes. Place in a 2-qt. serving bowl; drizzle with 1/3 cup orange juice. Chop chocolate; set aside 2 table-

spoons for garnish. Sprinkle remaining chocolate and 1 cup coconut over cake.

In a mixing bowl, combine milk, half-and-half, pudding mix and remaining orange juice; beat on low for 2 minutes. Spoon over cake. Sprinkle with remaining coconut and reserved chocolate. Refrigerate for at least 4 hours before serving. **Yield:** 10-14 servings.

Black Forest Trifle

(Pictured below)

When I want a dessert that's fit for a feast, I turn to this trifle. The recipe calls for a convenient brownie mix, so it's simple to make. —Peggy Linton
Cobourg, Ontario

- **1 package brownie mix (13-inch x 9-inch pan size)**
- **2 packages (2.8 ounces** *each***) chocolate mousse mix**
- **1 can (21 ounces) cherry pie filling**
- **1 carton (16 ounces) frozen whipped topping, thawed**
- **4 Skor candy bars, crushed**

Prepare and bake brownies according to package directions; cool completely on a wire rack. Prepare mousse according to package directions.

Crumble brownies; sprinkle half into a 4-qt. trifle dish or glass bowl. Top with half of the pie filling, mousse, whipped topping and candy bars. Repeat layers. Cover and refrigerate for 8 hours or overnight. **Yield:** 16 servings.

Snowy Cherry Trifles

I rely on store-bought angel food cake, canned pie filling and a few other convenience items for swift preparation. It's a great fast dessert with a festive look. To save even more time, layer it in a large glass bowl instead of making individual servings.
—May Evans, Corinth, Kentucky

    4 ounces cream cheese, softened
    1/4 cup sugar
    2 tablespoons milk
    1-3/4 cups whipped topping
    4 cups cubed angel food cake
    1 cup cherry pie filling
    1/4 teaspoon almond extract

In a large mixing bowl, beat the cream cheese and sugar. Add milk; beat until smooth. Fold in whipped topping and cake cubes. Transfer to individual serving dishes. Combine pie filling and almond extract; spoon over cake mixture. Refrigerate until serving. **Yield:** 4 servings.

Strawberry Tiramisu Trifle

We do a lot of entertaining. I like to make this easy trifle when I want to impress people. Berries make it different from a traditional tiramisu.
—Tammy Irvine, Whitby, Ontario

    1 quart fresh strawberries
    1-1/4 cups cold milk
    1 package (3.4 ounces) instant vanilla
      pudding mix
    1 package (8 ounces) cream cheese,
      softened
    4 tablespoons strong brewed coffee,
      room temperature, *divided*
    2 cups whipped topping
    1 package (3 ounces) ladyfingers, split
    6 squares (1 ounce *each*) bittersweet
      chocolate, grated

Set aside three strawberries for garnish; slice the remaining strawberries. In a bowl, whisk milk and pudding mix for 2 minutes. Let stand for 2 minutes or until soft-set. In a large mixing bowl, beat cream cheese until smooth; gradually beat in 2 tablespoons coffee. Beat in pudding. Fold in whipped topping.

Brush remaining coffee over ladyfingers. Line the bottom of a 3-qt. trifle or glass serving bowl with half of the ladyfingers. Top with half of the sliced berries, grated chocolate and pudding mixture; repeat layers. Cut reserved berries in half; place on trifle. Cover and refrigerate for 4 hours or overnight. **Yield:** 12 servings.

Chocolate Pineapple Trifle

We have this dessert every Christmas Day. Sometimes I'll serve individual helpings in stemmed goblets for an elegant holiday look. *—Gloria Vrabel Webster, Massachusetts*

    1 package (16 ounces) angel food cake
      mix
    1/2 cup sugar
    2 tablespoons cornstarch
    4 cups cold milk, *divided*
    3 eggs, lightly beaten
    1 can (20 ounces) crushed pineapple,
      drained
    1 teaspoon vanilla extract
    1 package (5.9 ounces) instant chocolate
      pudding mix
    1/3 cup water
    2 teaspoons rum extract
    2 cups heavy whipping cream
    2 tablespoons confectioners' sugar
Pineapple chunks and grated chocolate,
  optional

Prepare and bake cake according to package directions. Cool completely. Meanwhile, for pudding, combine sugar and cornstarch in a large saucepan. Gradually whisk in 2 cups of milk. Bring to a boil; cook and stir for 2 minutes or until thickened. Remove from heat. Stir 1/2 cup hot mixture into eggs; return all to pan, stirring constantly. Bring to a gentle boil; cook and stir 2 minutes longer.

Remove from the heat; stir in pineapple and vanilla. Pour into a bowl; press a piece of waxed paper or plastic wrap on top of pudding. Refrigerate, without stirring, until cooled. Meanwhile, place the remaining milk in a bowl. Whisk in chocolate pudding mix for 2 minutes or until thickened. Chill.

To assemble, cut cooled cake into 1-in. cubes. Place a third of the cake in a 3-1/2-qt. trifle dish. Combine water and rum extract; drizzle a third over the cake. Top with pineapple pudding, a third of the cake and a third of the rum mixture. Layer with the chocolate pudding and remaining cake and rum mixture. Cover and chill.

Just before serving, in a mixing bowl, beat cream and confectioners' sugar until stiff peaks form; spread over cake. Garnish with pineapple and grated chocolate if desired. **Yield:** 10-12 servings.

Textbook Trifles

Originally from England, trifles consisted of sponge cake or ladyfingers that were doused with spirits (usually sherry), covered with jam and custard, topped with whipped cream and garnished with fruit, nuts or grated chocolate.

Pies, Tarts
& Cobblers

German Plum Tart, p. 70

Apricot Meringue Pie

(Pictured below)

My sister-in-law wanted to create an apricot pie recipe, so we experimented until we came up with a combination of ingredients we liked. The meringue sits nice and high, while the sweet apricots retain a little of their chewy texture. It's yummy!
—Olive Rumage, Jacksboro, Texas

12 ounces dried apricots, chopped
1-1/2 cups water
2-1/2 cups sugar, *divided*
  3 tablespoons cornstarch
1/4 teaspoon salt
  4 eggs, *separated*
  2 tablespoons butter
1/4 teaspoon cream of tartar
  1 pastry shell (9 inches), baked

In a saucepan, bring apricots and water to a boil. Reduce heat; simmer, uncovered, for 10 minutes or until apricots are softened. In a bowl, combine 2 cups sugar, cornstarch and salt; stir into apricot mixture. Bring to a boil. Reduce heat; cook and stir for 1 minute or until thickened.

Remove from the heat; stir a small amount of hot filling into yolks. Return all to pan, stirring constantly. Bring to a gentle boil; cook and stir 1 minute longer or until glossy and clear. Remove from the heat; stir in butter. Keep warm.

In a mixing bowl, beat egg whites and cream of tartar on medium speed until soft peaks form. Gradually beat in remaining sugar, 1 tablespoon at a time, on high until stiff glossy peaks form and sugar is dissolved. Pour hot filling into crust. Spread meringue evenly over filling, sealing edges to crust.

Bake at 325° for 25-30 minutes or until golden brown. Cool on a wire rack for 1 hour. Chill for at least 3 hours before serving. Refrigerate leftovers.
Yield: 6-8 servings.

Almond Pear Tartlets

Although they're quick to fix, these pretty pastries are best when savored slowly. Delicately spiced pears are complemented by an almond sauce.
—Marie Rizzio, Traverse City, Michigan

  1 egg, lightly beaten
1/2 cup plus 6 tablespoons sugar, *divided*
3/4 cup heavy whipping cream
  2 tablespoons butter, melted
1/2 teaspoon almond extract
  1 package (10 ounces) frozen puff pastry
    shells, thawed
  2 small ripe pears, peeled and thinly
    sliced
1/2 teaspoon ground cinnamon
1/8 teaspoon ground ginger
1/2 cup slivered almonds, toasted, optional

In a saucepan, combine the egg, 1/2 cup sugar, cream and butter. Cook and stir until the sauce is thickened and a thermometer reads 160°. Remove from the heat; stir in extract. Cover and refrigerate.

On an unfloured surface, roll each pastry into a 4-in. circle. Place in an ungreased 15-in. x 10-in. x 1-in. baking pan. Top each with pear slices. Combine cinnamon, ginger and remaining sugar; sprinkle over pears. Bake at 400° for 20 minutes or until pastry is golden brown. Sprinkle with almonds if desired. Serve warm with the chilled cream sauce.
Yield: 6 servings.

Creamy Watermelon Pie

Cubes of sweet watermelon "float" in a creamy filling, made from condensed milk and whipped topping with a hint of lime.   —Brent Harrison
Nogales, Arizona

  1 can (14 ounces) sweetened condensed
    milk
1/4 cup lime juice

1-2/3 cups whipped topping
     2 cups cubed seeded watermelon
     1 graham cracker crust (9 inches)
Watermelon balls and fresh mint, optional

In a bowl, combine milk and lime juice; fold in whipped topping and cubed watermelon. Pour into crust. Refrigerate for at least 2 hours before slicing. Garnish with watermelon balls and mint if desired. **Yield:** 6-8 servings.

Almond Mocha Pie

I received this recipe from an aunt years ago, and have made it often since. The creamy chocolate pie—with a hint of coffee—is nice to have in the freezer for a quick reward on a hectic day.
     —Edna Johnson, St. Croix Falls, Wisconsin

     1 teaspoon instant coffee granules
     2 tablespoons boiling water
     1 milk chocolate candy bar with almonds
        (7 ounces)
     1 carton (8 ounces) frozen whipped
        topping, thawed
     1 pastry shell (9 inches), baked
Chocolate curls and additional whipped
     topping, optional

In a small bowl, dissolve coffee in boiling water; set aside. In a microwave or saucepan, melt the candy bar; cool slightly. Fold in half of the whipped topping. Fold in coffee and remaining whipped topping. Pour into pastry shell; freeze.

Remove the pie from the freezer about 15 minutes before serving. Garnish with chocolate curls and additional whipped topping if desired. **Yield:** 6-8 servings.

Country Plum Crumble

(Pictured above right)

My grandmother shared this recipe with me over 30 years ago. It was one of her favorites, and it always earned her compliments. —Shari Dore
     Brantford, Ontario

     1 cup canned plums, drained
     1/4 cup all-purpose flour
     1/4 cup sugar
     1/8 teaspoon salt
     1/8 teaspoon ground nutmeg
     1/4 cup cold butter

1/2 cup crushed cornflakes
Half-and-half cream, optional

Cut the plums in half; discard pits. Divide equally between four well-greased 6-oz. custard cups. In a bowl, combine the flour, sugar, salt and nutmeg; cut in butter until mixture is crumbly. Stir in cornflakes; sprinkle over plums.

Bake at 350° for 40 minutes or until the topping is golden brown. Serve warm with cream if desired. **Yield:** 4 servings.

Making Meringue

Eggs separate most cleanly when they are cold. After separating, place the whites in a small clean metal or glass mixing bowl and let stand at room temperature for 20-30 minutes.

Adding cream of tartar or another acidic ingredient before beating the whites is important—it stabilizes the egg white foam.

After stiff peaks form, check that the sugar is dissolved. It will feel silky smooth when rubbed between your thumb and index finger.

Spread the meringue over hot filling to minimize "weeping." Use a metal spatula to seal meringue to edges of pastry.

White Chocolate Fruit Tart

(Pictured above)

It takes a little time to make, but this tart is absolutely marvelous, especially in summer.
—Claire Darby, New Castle, Delaware

3/4 cup butter, softened
1/2 cup confectioners' sugar
1-1/2 cups all-purpose flour
FILLING:
    1 package (10 ounces) vanilla *or* white
      chips, melted
    1/4 cup heavy whipping cream
    1 package (8 ounces) cream cheese,
      softened
    1 can (20 ounces) pineapple chunks,
      undrained
    1 pint fresh strawberries, sliced
    1 can (11 ounces) mandarin oranges,
      drained
    2 kiwifruit, peeled and sliced
GLAZE:
    3 tablespoons sugar
    2 teaspoons cornstarch
    1/2 teaspoon lemon juice

In a mixing bowl, cream butter and sugar. Gradually add flour; mix well. Press into an ungreased 11-in. tart pan or 12-in. pizza pan with sides. Bake at 300° for 25-30 minutes or until lightly browned. Cool completely.

In a mixing bowl, beat chips and cream. Add cream cheese and beat until smooth. Spread over crust. Chill for 30 minutes. Drain pineapple, reserving 1/2 cup juice; set juice aside. Arrange strawberries, pineapple, oranges and kiwi over filling.

In a saucepan, combine sugar, cornstarch, lemon juice and reserved pineapple juice; bring to a boil over medium heat. Boil for 2 minutes or until thickened, stirring constantly. Cool; brush over fruit. Chill 1 hour before serving. Store in the refrigerator. **Yield:** 12-16 servings.

Raspberry Ribbon Pie

It's fun to go out as a family and pick raspberries to make my mother-in-law's pie recipe. We always freeze some berries, so we can make this pie year-round. —Anita Ohlson, Oak Harbor, Washington

1 cup vanilla wafer crumbs
1/4 cup butter, melted
    1 package (3 ounces) raspberry gelatin
    1 cup boiling water
1/4 cup sugar

1 cup fresh raspberries
1 tablespoon lemon juice
1 package (3 ounces) cream cheese, softened
1/3 cup confectioners' sugar
1 teaspoon vanilla extract
Pinch salt
1 cup heavy whipping cream
Additional whipped cream and fresh raspberries

In a bowl, combine the wafer crumbs and butter; press onto the bottom and up the sides of an ungreased 9-in. pie plate. Bake at 350° for 10 minutes or until golden brown.

In a bowl, dissolve gelatin in boiling water. Add the sugar, raspberries and lemon juice. Refrigerate until partially set, about 1-1/2 hours.

In a mixing bowl, beat cream cheese and confectioners' sugar until smooth. Add vanilla and salt. In another mixing bowl, beat whipping cream until stiff peaks form. Fold into the cream cheese mixture.

Spread 3/4 cup over bottom of crust. Spread 3/4 cup raspberry mixture over the top; repeat layers. Refrigerate for 8 hours or overnight before serving. Garnish pie with additional whipped cream and berries. **Yield:** 6-8 servings.

Cherry Blueberry Pie

Southwestern Michigan is noted for its fruit. I experimented and came up with this pie recipe that combines cherries and blueberries. It's especially good served warm with ice cream. —Betty Williams Scotts, Michigan

Pastry for a double-crust pie (9 inches)
2 cups pitted sweet cherries
2 cups fresh blueberries
3/4 cup sugar
1/4 cup all-purpose flour
1/8 teaspoon ground nutmeg
1 tablespoon butter
Additional sugar

Line a 9-in. pie plate with bottom crust; trim pastry even with edge. Set aside. In a bowl, gently combine cherries and blueberries. Combine the sugar, flour and nutmeg; stir into fruit. Let stand for 10 minutes. Pour into crust; dot with butter. Roll out remaining pastry; make a lattice crust. Seal and flute edges. Sprinkle with sugar. Cover edges of pastry loosely with foil.

Bake at 425° for 15 minutes. Reduce heat to 350°; bake 30-35 minutes longer or until pastry is golden brown and filling is bubbly. Cool on a wire rack. **Yield:** 6-8 servings.

Old-Fashioned Apple Crisp

(Pictured below)

Now young adults, our children say this dessert is "awesome" with ice cream. Everyone who takes a bite nods in agreement! Nostalgic, comforting, luscious—call it what you will, this is one of those simple, old-time treats that never goes out of style.
—Grace Yaskovic
Branchville, New Jersey

4 cups sliced peeled tart apples (about 3 medium)
3/4 cup packed brown sugar
1/2 cup all-purpose flour
1/2 cup rolled oats
1 teaspoon ground cinnamon
1/4 to 1/2 teaspoon ground allspice
1/3 cup cold butter
Vanilla ice cream, optional

Place apples in a greased 8-in. square baking dish. In a bowl, combine brown sugar, flour, oats, cinnamon and allspice; cut in butter until crumbly. Sprinkle over apples. Bake at 375° for 30-35 minutes or until apples are tender. Serve warm with ice cream if desired. **Yield:** 4-6 servings.

Macadamia Caramel Tart

(Pictured below)

Knowing my co-workers are willing guinea pigs, I tried this recipe for an office potluck. When I returned from a break, I found a big frilly blue ribbon on my desk with a note from the boss, saying, "You get a blue ribbon for bringing us a 'slice of heaven'!"
—Debbie Emerick
Castle Rock, Colorado

2-3/4 cups all-purpose flour
2-1/2 cups sugar, *divided*
  1 cup cold butter, cut into chunks
  2 eggs
  1 cup heavy whipping cream
2-1/2 cups macadamia nuts, toasted
  1 egg white, beaten

In a food processor, combine flour, 1/2 cup sugar and butter. Cover; pulse until blended. Add eggs; pulse until blended. On a lightly floured surface, gently knead dough 5 times or until a ball forms.

Between two sheets of waxed paper, roll two-thirds of dough into a 13-in. circle; press onto the bottom and 2 in. up the sides of an ungreased 9-in. springform pan. Cover and chill. Roll remaining dough into a 9-in. circle; chill.

In a large heavy skillet, cook and stir the remaining sugar over medium heat until melted and dark brown, about 20 minutes. Slowly stir in cream until blended. Remove from the heat; stir in nuts. Cool for 15 minutes. Pour into prepared pan. Top with 9-in. pastry circle. Fold pastry from sides of pan over the top pastry; seal edges with a fork. Brush top with egg white.

Bake at 325° for 50-55 minutes or until golden brown. Cool on a wire rack for 20 minutes. Carefully run a knife around edge of pan to loosen. Remove sides of pan. Cool completely before cutting. **Yield:** 10-12 servings.

Nectarine Cream Pie

This is a good dessert on hot summer days like we have here in Florida. It's cool and cheery, and it also tastes yummy!
—Marilyn Day
North Fort Meyers, Florida

  1 cup sliced fresh *or* **frozen unsweetened strawberries, thawed**
1/2 cup sugar
  1 tablespoon cornstarch
1/4 cup water
  1 tablespoon lemon juice
Red food coloring, optional
  2 packages (3 ounces *each***) cream cheese, softened**
  1 cup confectioners' sugar
1/4 teaspoon almond extract
  1 cup heavy whipping cream, whipped
  1 pastry shell (9 inches), baked
  2 cups sliced peeled fresh *or* **frozen nectarines, thawed**

In a bowl, mash the strawberries. In a saucepan, combine the sugar, cornstarch and water until blended; stir in mashed berries. Bring to a boil; cook and stir for 2 minutes or until thickened. Remove from the heat; stir in lemon juice and food coloring if desired. Cool.

In a small mixing bowl, beat the cream cheese, confectioners' sugar and extract until smooth. Fold in whipped cream. Spoon into the pastry shell. Arrange nectarines over cream mixture. Top with strawberry mixture. Refrigerate until set, about 3 hours. **Yield:** 6-8 servings.

Walnut Apple Pie

Adding walnuts gives a slight twist to traditional apple pie recipes and adds a unique flavor we enjoy.
—Diane Laverty, Marysville, Pennsylvania

  4 to 5 large tart apples, peeled and sliced
  1 tablespoon lemon juice
1/2 cup sugar
1/4 cup packed brown sugar
1/2 cup chopped walnuts
  2 tablespoons quick-cooking tapioca
1/2 teaspoon ground cinnamon
1/4 teaspoon ground nutmeg

Pastry for double-crust pie (9 inches)
    2 tablespoons butter

In a bowl, toss apples with lemon juice. Combine the sugars, nuts, tapioca, cinnamon and nutmeg; add to apples and toss to coat. Let mixture stand for 15 minutes.

Line a 9-in. pie plate with bottom pastry; trim even with edge. Add apple mixture; dot with butter. Roll out remaining pastry to fit top of pie; place over filling. Trim, seal and flute edges. Cut slits in top. Cover edges loosely with foil. Bake at 400° for 40-45 minutes or until crust is brown and filling is bubbly. Cool on a wire rack. **Yield:** 6-8 servings.

Pear Crisp with Lemon Sauce

Everyone loves the crunchy oat topping and sweet pear filling in this fruity crisp. —Rachel Franklin
Hockley, Texas

  2 tablespoons plus 1/4 cup all-purpose flour, *divided*
  1 tablespoon sugar
  1 teaspoon grated lemon peel, *divided*
  5 cups sliced peeled ripe pears (about 2 pounds)
  1/2 cup old-fashioned oats
  1/4 cup packed brown sugar
  1/8 teaspoon ground cardamom
  3 tablespoons cold butter
  1/4 cup sliced almonds
LEMON SAUCE:
  1/4 cup sugar
  2 teaspoons cornstarch
  1/2 cup cold water
  1 egg yolk, beaten
  1 tablespoon butter
  1 tablespoon lemon juice
  1/4 teaspoon grated lemon peel

In a large bowl, combine 2 tablespoons flour, sugar and 1/4 teaspoon of lemon peel. Add pears; gently toss to coat. Transfer to a greased 8-in. square baking dish. Combine the oats, brown sugar, cardamom and remaining flour and lemon peel; mix well. Cut in butter until mixture resembles coarse crumbs. Stir in almonds. Sprinkle over pears. Bake at 375° for 35-40 minutes or until pears are tender and topping is golden brown.

For lemon sauce, combine sugar and cornstarch in a saucepan. Gradually stir in water until smooth. Bring to a boil over medium heat; cook and stir for 1 minute or until thickened. Remove from the heat.

Stir a small amount of hot mixture into egg yolk; return all to pan, stirring constantly. Bring to a

gentle boil over medium heat. Cook and stir 1 minute longer. Remove from the heat; stir in butter, lemon juice and peel. Serve with warm pear crisp. **Yield:** 9 servings.

Mom's Custard Pie

(Pictured above)

Just a single bite of this traditional treat takes me back to the days when Mom would fix this pie for Dad, Grandfather and me. —Barbara Hyatt
Folsom, California

  1 unbaked pastry shell (9 inches)
  4 eggs
  1/2 cup sugar
  1/4 teaspoon salt
  1 teaspoon vanilla extract
2-1/2 cups milk
  1/4 teaspoon ground nutmeg

Line unpricked pastry shell with a double thickness of heavy-duty foil. Bake at 450° for 8 minutes. Remove foil; bake 5 minutes longer. Remove from the oven and set aside.

Separate one egg; set the white aside. In a mixing bowl, beat the yolk and remaining eggs just until combined. Blend in sugar, salt and vanilla. Stir in milk. Beat reserved egg white until stiff peaks form; fold into egg mixture. Carefully pour into crust. Cover edges of pie with foil.

Bake at 350° for 25 minutes. Remove foil; bake 15-20 minutes longer or until a knife inserted near the center comes out clean. Cool on a wire rack. Sprinkle with nutmeg. Store in the refrigerator. **Yield:** 6-8 servings.

Apple Rhubarb Crumble

Here in Vermont, we enjoy a bounty of rhubarb, apples and maple syrup. These ingredients inspired me to create this dessert. —Liz Bachilas
Shelburne, Vermont

    3 **cups chopped fresh** *or* **frozen rhubarb**
    2 **medium tart apples, peeled and chopped**
    1 **egg**
3/4 **cup sugar**
1/4 **cup maple syrup**
1/4 **to 1/2 teaspoon ground nutmeg**
1/4 **teaspoon ground cinnamon**
    1 **cup all-purpose flour**
1/2 **cup packed brown sugar**
Pinch salt
1/2 **cup cold butter**

In a bowl, combine the rhubarb, apples, egg, sugar, syrup, nutmeg and cinnamon. Pour into a greased 2-qt. baking dish. In another bowl, combine the flour, brown sugar and salt. Cut in butter until the mixture resembles coarse crumbs; sprinkle over fruit mixture. Bake at 350° for 45-55 minutes or until bubbly. **Yield:** 4-6 servings.

Chocolate Mallow Pie

(Pictured above)

This rich and fudgy cream cheese pie should serve eight, but it never does because so many folks request a second slice! I've been cooking for more than 60 years...and this is the best chocolate pie recipe I've found. —Louise Genn
Cosmopolis, Washington

1-1/4 **cups crushed cream-filled chocolate sandwich cookies (about 14 cookies)**
  1/4 **cup butter, melted**
    2 **tablespoons sugar**
    2 **packages (one 8 ounces, one 3 ounces) cream cheese, softened**
  1/2 **cup chocolate syrup**
1-1/3 **cups semisweet chocolate chips, melted**
    1 **carton (8 ounces) frozen whipped topping, thawed**
    2 **cups miniature marshmallows**
Chocolate curls, optional

In a bowl, combine the cookie crumbs, butter and sugar. Press onto the bottom and up the sides of a 9-in. pie plate. Bake at 375° for 8-10 minutes or until set; cool completely on a wire rack.
   In a mixing bowl, beat cream cheese and chocolate syrup until blended. Beat in melted chips. Set aside 1/4 cup of whipped topping. Fold marshmallows and remaining whipped topping into chocolate mixture. Spoon into crust. Refrigerate for at least 8 hours or overnight. Garnish with reserved whipped topping and chocolate curls if desired. **Yield:** 8 servings.

Mountainous Mandarin Pie

As a chocolate lover, I created this creamy chocolate and orange pie to satisfy my cravings. When I served it to friends, they each polished off one piece and asked for seconds. —Shelly Platten
Amherst, Wisconsin

    1 **package (8 ounces) cream cheese, softened**
    1 **can (14 ounces) sweetened condensed milk**
  1/2 **cup orange juice concentrate**
  1/2 **cup sour cream**
    2 **drops yellow food coloring, optional**
    1 **drop red food coloring, optional**
    1 **carton (8 ounces) frozen whipped topping, thawed**
    1 **chocolate crumb crust (9 inches)**
    1 **can (15 ounces) mandarin oranges, drained**
    1 **square (1 ounce) unsweetened chocolate**
    1 **teaspoon shortening**

In a mixing bowl, beat cream cheese until fluffy. Add the milk, orange juice concentrate, sour cream and food coloring if desired; beat until smooth. Fold in the whipped topping. Spoon half into crust. Set eight mandarin orange segments aside. Arrange remaining oranges over filling. Top with remaining filling and reserved oranges.

In a microwave, melt chocolate and shortening. Stir until smooth; cool slightly. Drizzle over pie. Chill for at least 4 hours before slicing. **Yield:** 6-8 servings.

Frost-on-the-Pumpkin Pie

Like the spices in traditional pumpkin pie? Then try this tasty twist. Most people make this cool fluffy version for the holidays, but I think it's wonderful any time of year. —Tammy Covey
Huntington, Arkansas

1-1/2 cups graham cracker crumbs (about 24
    squares)
   3 tablespoons sugar
1/4 teaspoon ground nutmeg
1/8 teaspoon ground cloves
1/3 cup butter, melted
FILLING:
   1 can (16 ounces) vanilla frosting
   1 can (15 ounces) solid-pack pumpkin
   1 cup (8 ounces) sour cream
   1 to 1-1/2 teaspoons ground cinnamon
1/2 to 1 teaspoon ground ginger
1/4 to 1/2 teaspoon ground cloves
   1 cup whipped topping

In a small bowl, combine the first five ingredients. Set aside 1 tablespoon for topping. Press remaining crumb mixture onto the bottom and up the sides of an ungreased 9-in. pie plate. Bake at 350° for 7-9 minutes or until crust just begins to brown. Cool on a wire rack.

In a mixing bowl, combine frosting, pumpkin, sour cream, cinnamon, ginger and cloves. Fold in whipped topping. Spoon into the crust. Sprinkle with the reserved crumb mixture. Refrigerate for at least 4 hours before serving. **Yield:** 6-8 servings.

Strawberry Satin Pie

(Pictured at right)

My mom loved to spoil us with tempting desserts like this pretty springtime treat. Toasted sliced almonds sprinkled over the bottom crust, a smooth-as-satin filling and a lovely strawberry glaze make this a memorable pie. —Lorrie Bailey
Pulaski, Iowa

   1 pastry shell (9 inches), baked
1/2 cup sliced almonds, toasted
1/2 cup sugar
   3 tablespoons all-purpose flour

   3 tablespoons cornstarch
1/2 teaspoon salt
   2 cups milk
   1 egg, lightly beaten
   1 teaspoon vanilla extract
1/2 cup heavy whipping cream, whipped
GLAZE:
   3 cups fresh strawberries
   1 cup water
1/3 cup sugar
   2 tablespoons cornstarch
  12 drops red food coloring, optional

Cover bottom of pie shell with almonds; set aside. In a saucepan, combine the sugar, flour, cornstarch and salt. Stir in milk until smooth. Bring to a boil; cook and stir for 2 minutes or until thickened.

Remove from the heat. Stir a small amount of hot filling into egg. Return all to the pan, stirring constantly. Bring to a gentle boil; cook and stir 2 minutes longer. Remove from the heat. Stir in vanilla. Cool to room temperature. Whisk in whipped cream until blended. Pour into pie shell. Cover and refrigerate for at least 2 hours.

Crush 1 cup of strawberries; set remaining berries aside. In a saucepan, bring crushed berries and water to a boil; cook, uncovered, for 2 minutes. Strain through cheesecloth; discard fruit and set liquid aside to cool.

In another saucepan, combine sugar and cornstarch; gradually stir in berry liquid until blended. Bring to a boil; cook and stir for 2 minutes or until thickened. Stir in food coloring if desired. Cool for 20 minutes. Slice the reserved strawberries; arrange over chilled filling. Pour glaze evenly over berries. Refrigerate for at least 1 hour before serving. **Yield:** 6-8 servings.

Lemon Tart

(Pictured below)

Here's a luscious way to end a meal! Smooth and creamy, with a refreshing lemon taste, this tart gets rave reviews. Every time I serve it to someone new, it results in a request for the recipe.

—Erlene Cornelius
Spring City, Tennessee

1 cup sugar
1/4 cup cornstarch
1 cup milk
3 egg yolks, beaten
1/4 cup butter
1 tablespoon grated lemon peel
1/3 cup lemon juice
1 cup (8 ounces) sour cream
1 pastry shell (9 inches), baked
Whipped topping

In a saucepan, combine the sugar and cornstarch. Gradually add milk until smooth. Cook and stir over medium-high heat until thickened. Reduce heat; cook and stir 2 minutes longer.

Remove from the heat. Stir a small amount of hot liquid into egg yolks; return all to the pan. Bring to a gentle boil, stirring constantly. Cook 2 minutes longer (mixture will be very thick).

Remove from the heat; stir in the butter and lemon peel. Gently stir in the lemon juice. Cover and cool completely. Fold in the sour cream. Pour into the pastry shell. Refrigerate for at least 2 hours before cutting. Garnish with whipped topping. **Yield:** 6-8 servings.

Crustless Pineapple Pie

I took a favorite pie recipe and substituted canned pineapple for the coconut it called for. The results were delicious. —Christi Ross, Guthrie, Texas

2 cups milk
2/3 cup sugar
1/2 cup biscuit/baking mix
1/4 cup butter, melted
2 eggs
1-1/2 teaspoons vanilla extract
Yellow food coloring, optional
2 cans (8 ounces *each*) crushed pineapple, well drained
Whipped topping, optional

In a blender, combine the milk, sugar, biscuit mix, butter, eggs, vanilla and food coloring if desired; cover and process until smooth. Sprinkle the pineapple into a greased deep-dish 9-in. pie plate. Pour batter over pineapple.

Bake at 350° for 40-45 minutes or until a knife inserted near the center comes out clean. Garnish with whipped topping if desired. **Yield:** 6-8 servings.

Creamy Banana Pecan Pie

I always get compliments when I serve this layered banana beauty. —Isabel Fowler
Fairbanks, Alaska

1 cup all-purpose flour
1/2 cup butter, softened
1 cup finely chopped pecans
1 package (8 ounces) cream cheese, softened
1 cup confectioners' sugar
1 carton (8 ounces) frozen whipped topping, thawed, *divided*
3 large firm bananas, sliced
1 package (3.4 ounces) instant vanilla pudding mix
1-1/3 cups cold milk
Additional chopped pecans, optional

Combine flour, butter and pecans. Press onto bottom and up sides of a greased 9-in. pie plate. Bake at 350° for 25 minutes. Cool completely.

In a mixing bowl, beat cream cheese and sugar. Fold in 1 cup of whipped topping. Spread over the crust. Arrange bananas on top. In a bowl, whisk pudding mix and milk. Immediately pour over bananas. Top with remaining whipped topping. Garnish with pecans if desired. Refrigerate until serving. **Yield:** 6-8 servings.

Cherry Tarts

At our house, we celebrate George Washington's birthday with this cherry dessert.
—Verna Burkholder, Dorchester, Wisconsin

1-1/2 cups all-purpose flour
1/2 teaspoon salt
1/2 cup shortening
  4 to 5 tablespoons cold water
3/4 cup sugar
  3 tablespoons cornstarch
  2 cans (14-1/2 ounces *each***) pitted tart cherries**
  1 tablespoon butter
1/4 teaspoon almond extract
  4 to 5 drops red food coloring, optional

In a bowl, combine the flour and salt. Cut in shortening until mixture resembles coarse crumbs. Add enough water until dough forms a ball. Refrigerate for 30 minutes.

On a lightly floured surface, roll out dough to 1/8-in. thickness. Cut out eight 5-in. circles. Place each over an inverted custard cup on an ungreased 15-in. x 10-in. x 1-in. baking pan. Bake at 450° for 10-11 minutes or until golden brown. Cool for 5 minutes before removing tart shells from custard cups; cool completely on wire racks.

For filling, in a saucepan, combine the sugar and cornstarch. Drain cherries, reserving 1 cup juice. Set cherries aside. Stir reserved juice into the sugar mixture until smooth. Bring to a boil; cook and stir for 2 minutes or until thickened. Remove from the heat; stir in the cherries, butter, almond extract and food coloring if desired. Cool to room temperature. Spoon about 1/4 cup filling into each tart shell. **Yield:** 8 servings.

Coconut Cream Meringue Pie

(Pictured above right)

We usually have a good selection of pies at our neighborhood get-togethers, but I always come home with an empty pan when I bring this classic. Friends line up for a creamy slice, topped with golden meringue and toasted coconut.
—Betty Sitzman, Wray, Colorado

  2/3 cup sugar
1/4 cup cornstarch
1/4 teaspoon salt
  2 cups milk
  3 egg yolks, lightly beaten
  1 cup flaked coconut, finely chopped
  2 tablespoons butter
1/2 teaspoon vanilla extract
MERINGUE:
  3 egg whites
1/4 teaspoon cream of tartar
  6 tablespoons sugar
  1 pastry shell (9 inches), baked
1/2 cup flaked coconut

In a saucepan, combine the sugar, cornstarch and salt. Gradually stir in milk until smooth. Bring to a boil; cook and stir for 2 minutes or until thickened. Gradually stir 1 cup hot filling into egg yolks; return all to the pan, stirring constantly. Bring to a gentle boil; cook and stir for 2 minutes. Remove from the heat; stir in chopped coconut, butter and vanilla until butter is melted.

For meringue, in a mixing bowl, beat the egg whites on medium speed until foamy. Add cream of tartar; beat until soft peaks form. Gradually beat in sugar, 1 tablespoon at a time, on high until stiff peaks form.

Pour hot filling into crust. Spread with meringue, sealing edges to crust. Sprinkle with flaked coconut. Bake at 350° for 13-15 minutes or until golden brown. Cool on a wire rack for 1 hour; chill for 1-2 hours before serving. Refrigerate leftovers. **Yield:** 6-8 servings.

Zucchini Crisp

An avid gardener, my husband, Jamie, hates to see any of his work go to waste. So we fix this dessert that tastes like it's made with apples but uses up a bounty of zucchini. It's so good, even those who don't like vegetables enjoy it. —Deborah Trescott
Marianna, Florida

    8 cups cubed peeled zucchini
    3/4 cup lemon juice
    1/2 to 3/4 cup sugar
    2 teaspoons ground cinnamon
    1 teaspoon ground nutmeg
TOPPING:
1-1/3 cups packed brown sugar
    1 cup old-fashioned oats
    1 cup all-purpose flour
    2/3 cup cold butter

In a bowl, combine the zucchini, lemon juice, sugar, cinnamon and nutmeg; mix well. Pour into a greased 13-in. x 9-in. x 2-in. baking dish.

For topping, combine brown sugar, oats and flour in a bowl; cut in butter until crumbly. Sprinkle over the zucchini mixture. Bake at 375° for 45-50 minutes or until bubbly and the zucchini is tender. **Yield:** 12-15 servings.

Colorado Peach Cobbler

My husband and I have lived on our ranch/wheat farm for over 40 years. I've served this dessert for family, hired help and special guests many times. I've used other fruits that are in season, but we like peaches best. —Clara Hinman
Flagler, Colorado

    1 cup sugar
    2 tablespoons all-purpose flour
    1/4 teaspoon ground nutmeg
    4 cups sliced peeled fresh peaches
TOPPING:
    1 cup sugar
    1 cup all-purpose flour
    1 teaspoon baking powder
    1 teaspoon salt
    1/3 cup cold butter
    1 egg, beaten
Ice cream, optional

In a bowl, combine sugar, flour and nutmeg. Add peaches; stir to coat. Pour into a greased 11-in. x 7-in. x 2-in. baking pan.

For topping, combine the sugar, flour, baking powder and salt; cut in the butter until the mixture resembles fine crumbs. Stir in the egg. Spoon over the peaches.

Bake at 375° for 35-40 minutes or until filling is bubbly and topping is golden. Serve hot or cold with ice cream if desired. **Yield:** 8-10 servings.

German Plum Tart

(Pictured on page 59)

The buttery crust of this fruit-filled treat melts in your mouth. You can substitute sliced apples or peaches for the plums with great results. I've used this crust with blueberries, too. —Helga Schlape
Florham Park, New Jersey

    1/2 cup butter, softened
    4 tablespoons sugar, *divided*
    1 egg yolk
    3/4 to 1 cup all-purpose flour
    2 pounds plums, quartered (about 4 cups)

In a mixing bowl, cream butter and 3 tablespoons sugar until fluffy. Beat in egg yolk. Gradually add flour, 1/4 cup at a time, until mixture forms a soft dough. Press onto the bottom and up the sides of a 10-in. pie plate.

Arrange plums, skin side up with edges overlapping, in crust; sprinkle with remaining sugar. Bake at 350° for 35-45 minutes or until crust is golden brown and fruit is tender. **Yield:** 6-8 servings.

Peanut Butter Pie

This pie is always a treat at our house. I haven't met anyone who doesn't like it. —Gloria Pittman
Shelby, North Carolina

    1/3 cup creamy peanut butter
    1 package (3 ounces) cream cheese, softened
    2 tablespoons butter, softened
    1 cup confectioners' sugar
    1/4 cup milk
    1 carton (8 ounces) frozen whipped topping, thawed
    1 chocolate crumb crust (9 inches)
    2 tablespoons chopped peanuts, optional
Chocolate curls, optional

In a mixing bowl, beat peanut butter, cream cheese and butter until smooth. Add sugar and milk; fold in whipped topping. Pour into the crust.

Cover and freeze for at least 4 hours. Remove from the freezer just before serving. Garnish with peanuts and chocolate curls if desired. **Yield:** 6 servings.

Cheddar Pear Pie

Any way you slice it, pie is a terrific treat. Old-fashioned and traditional or unusual and deliciously different, the wonderful wedges delight senses and tempt taste buds.

The winners of our Pie Potpourri contest are no exception. Home cooks entered almost 5,000 pies with a vast variety of crusts and fillings.

Try our taste panel's picks in your kitchen—you'll find that getting sincere compliments is easy as pie!

At the top of this luscious lineup is Cheddar Pear Pie, picked as the Grand Prize Winner. Cynthia LaBree of Elmer, New Jersey shared the scrumptious dessert.

"I take this pie to lots of different gatherings, and I make sure to have copies of the recipe with me since people always ask for it," says Cynthia. "It's amusing to see some folks puzzling over what's in the filling—they expect apples but love the subtle sweetness of the pears."
> —Cynthia LaBree, Elmer, New Jersey

    4 large ripe pears, peeled and thinly sliced
1/3 cup sugar
1 tablespoon cornstarch
1/8 teaspoon salt
1 unbaked pastry shell (9 inches)
TOPPING:
    1/2 cup shredded cheddar cheese
1/2 cup all-purpose flour
1/4 cup butter, melted
1/4 cup sugar
1/4 teaspoon salt

In a bowl, combine pears, sugar, cornstarch and salt. Pour into pastry shell. Combine topping ingredients until crumbly; sprinkle over filling.

Bake at 425° for 25-35 minutes or until crust is golden and cheese is melted. Cool on a wire rack for 15-20 minutes. Serve warm. Store in the refrigerator. **Yield:** 6-8 servings.

Peanutty Ice Cream Pie

A friend gave me this recipe over 25 years ago. The unique crust makes these cool slices extra peanutty and perfect for a party. I keep the recipe handy, since it's great for any occasion.
> —Donna Cline, Pensacola, Florida

    1-1/3 cups finely chopped peanuts
3 tablespoons butter, melted
2 tablespoons sugar
FILLING:
    1/4 cup peanut butter
1/4 cup light corn syrup
1/4 cup flaked coconut
3 tablespoons chopped peanuts
1 quart vanilla ice cream, softened
Miniature M&M's or semisweet chocolate chips

Combine the peanuts, butter and sugar; press onto the bottom and up the sides of a greased 9-in. pie plate. Cover and refrigerate for 15 minutes.

In a large bowl, combine peanut butter and corn syrup. Add coconut and peanuts. Stir in ice cream just until combined. Spoon into crust. Cover and freeze overnight or until firm. Just before serving, sprinkle with M&M's or chocolate chips. **Yield:** 6-8 servings.

Chocolate Raspberry Pie

After tasting this pie at my sister-in-law's house, I had to have the recipe. I love the chocolate and raspberry layers separated by a dreamy cream layer.
—Ruth Bartel, Morris, Manitoba

1 unbaked pastry shell (9 inches)
3 tablespoons sugar
1 tablespoon cornstarch
2 cups fresh or frozen unsweetened
   raspberries, thawed
FILLING:
   1 package (8 ounces) cream cheese,
     softened
1/3 cup sugar
1/2 teaspoon vanilla extract
1/2 cup heavy whipping cream, whipped
TOPPING:
   2 squares (1 ounce each) semisweet
     chocolate
3 tablespoons butter

Line unpricked pastry shell with a double thickness of heavy-duty foil. Bake at 450° for 8 minutes. Remove foil; bake 5 minutes longer. Cool on a wire rack.

In a saucepan, combine sugar and cornstarch. Stir in the raspberries; bring to a boil over medium heat. Boil and stir for 2 minutes. Remove from the heat; cool for 15 minutes. Spread into shell; refrigerate.

In a mixing bowl, beat cream cheese, sugar and vanilla until fluffy. Fold in whipped cream. Carefully spread over raspberry layer. Cover and refrigerate for at least 1 hour.

Melt chocolate and butter; cool for 4-5 minutes. Pour over filling. Cover and chill for at least 2 hours. Store in the refrigerator. **Yield:** 6-8 servings.

Fluffy Caramel Pie

I bake a variety of pies, but this is the one my husband likes best. The gingersnap crumb crust is a tangy contrast to the sweet, lighter-than-air caramel filling.　*—Ginger Hendricksen,*
Wisconsin Rapids, Wisconsin

1-1/2 cups crushed gingersnaps (about 30
    cookies)
1/4 cup butter, melted
FILLING:
   1/4 cup cold water
   1 envelope unflavored gelatin
  28 caramels
   1 cup milk
Dash salt
   1/2 cup chopped pecans
   1 teaspoon vanilla extract
   1 cup heavy whipping cream, whipped
Caramel ice cream topping and additional
    pecans, optional

Combine the cookie crumbs and butter; press onto the bottom and up the sides of a greased 9-in. pie plate. Cover and chill.

Meanwhile, place cold water in a heavy saucepan; sprinkle with gelatin. Let stand for 1 minute. Add caramels, milk and salt; cook and stir over low heat until gelatin is dissolved and caramels are melted. Refrigerate for 1-2 hours or until mixture mounds when stirred with a spoon.

Stir in pecans and vanilla. Fold in whipped cream. Pour into crust. Refrigerate for 6 hours or overnight. Garnish with ice cream topping and pecans if desired. Store in the refrigerator. **Yield:** 6-8 servings.

Triple Fruit Pie

My goal is to create pies as good as my mother's. I came up with this recipe to use up fruit in my freezer. The first time I made it, my family begged for seconds. If I continue making pies this good, maybe someday our two daughters will be striving to imitate mine!

—Jeanne Freybler, Grand Rapids, Michigan

1-1/4 cups each fresh blueberries, raspberries and chopped rhubarb
1/2 teaspoon almond extract
1-1/4 cups sugar
1/4 cup quick-cooking tapioca
1/4 teaspoon ground nutmeg
1/4 teaspoon salt
1 tablespoon lemon juice
Pastry for double-crust pie (9 inches)

In a large bowl, combine fruits and extract; toss to coat. In another bowl, combine sugar, tapioca, nutmeg and salt. Add to fruit; stir gently. Let stand for 15 minutes.

Line a 9-in. pie plate with bottom crust; trim pastry even with edge. Stir lemon juice into fruit mixture; spoon into the crust. Roll out remaining pastry; make a lattice crust. Seal and flute edges.

Bake at 400° for 20 minutes. Reduce heat to 350°; bake 30 minutes longer or until the crust is golden brown and the filling is bubbly. **Yield:** 6-8 servings.

Editor's Note: Frozen berries and rhubarb may be substituted for fresh; thaw and drain before using.

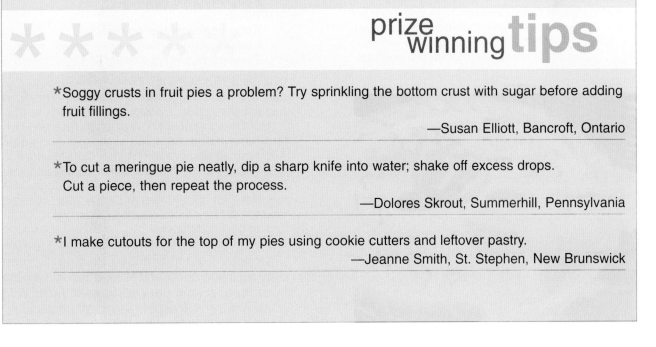

prize winning tips

*Soggy crusts in fruit pies a problem? Try sprinkling the bottom crust with sugar before adding fruit fillings.

—Susan Elliott, Bancroft, Ontario

*To cut a meringue pie neatly, dip a sharp knife into water; shake off excess drops. Cut a piece, then repeat the process.

—Dolores Skrout, Summerhill, Pennsylvania

*I make cutouts for the top of my pies using cookie cutters and leftover pastry.

—Jeanne Smith, St. Stephen, New Brunswick

Frosted Orange Pie

With its fresh-tasting filling and fluffy frosting, this pretty pie is truly an elegant final course.
—Delores Edgecomb, Atlanta, New York

- 3/4 cup sugar
- 1/2 cup all-purpose flour
- 1/4 teaspoon salt
- 1-1/4 cups water
- 2 egg yolks, lightly beaten
- 2 to 3 tablespoons grated orange peel
- 1/2 teaspoon grated lemon peel
- 1/2 cup orange juice
- 2 tablespoons lemon juice
- 1 pastry shell (9 inches), baked

FROSTING:
- 1/2 cup sugar
- 2 egg whites
- 2 tablespoons water
- 1/8 teaspoon each cream of tartar and salt
- 1/2 cup flaked coconut, toasted

In a saucepan, combine sugar, flour and salt; gradually add water. Cook and stir over medium-high heat for 2-3 minutes or until thickened and bubbly. Remove from heat. Gradually stir 1/2 cup into egg yolks; return all to pan. Bring to a gentle boil; cook and stir for 2 minutes. Remove from the heat; stir in orange peel and lemon peel. Gently stir in juices. Pour into pastry shell. Cool on a wire rack for 1 hour. Chill at least 3 hours.

In a heavy saucepan or double boiler, combine sugar, egg whites, water, cream of tartar and salt. With a portable mixer, beat on low speed for 1 minute. Continue beating on low over low heat until frosting reaches 160°, about 8-10 minutes.

With a stand mixer, beat on high until frosting forms stiff peaks, about 7 minutes. Spread over chilled pie. Just before serving, sprinkle with coconut. Store in the refrigerator. **Yield:** 6-8 servings.

Fudgy Pecan Pie

When I serve this chocolate pie, guests often tell me, "Your pie looks too good to eat—but I won't let that stop me!"
—Ellen Arndt, Cologne, Minnesota

- 1 unbaked pastry shell (9 inches)
- 1 package (4 ounces) German sweet chocolate
- 1/4 cup butter
- 1 can (14 ounces) sweetened condensed milk
- 1/2 cup water
- 2 eggs, beaten
- 1 teaspoon vanilla extract
- 1/4 teaspoon salt
- 1/2 cup chopped pecans

FILLING:
- 1 cup cold milk
- 1 package (3.9 ounces) instant chocolate pudding mix
- 1 cup whipped topping

TOPPING:
- 1 cup heavy whipping cream
- 1 tablespoon confectioners' sugar
- 1 teaspoon vanilla extract

Line unpricked pastry shell with double-thick heavy-duty foil. Bake at 450° for 5 minutes. Remove foil and set shell aside. Reduce heat to 375°.

In a heavy saucepan, melt chocolate and butter. Remove from the heat; stir in milk and water. Add a small amount of hot chocolate mixture to eggs; return all to the pan. Stir in vanilla and salt. Pour into shell; sprinkle with nuts. Cover edges with foil. Bake for 35 minutes or until a knife inserted near the center comes out clean. Remove to a wire rack to cool completely.

In a mixing bowl, beat milk and pudding mix until smooth. Fold in whipped topping. Spread over nut layer; cover and refrigerate. In a mixing bowl, beat cream until soft peaks form. Add sugar and vanilla, beating until stiff peaks form. Spread over pudding layer. Refrigerate until set, about 4 hours. **Yield:** 6-8 servings.

Puddings &
Parfaits

Minty Cocoa Mousse, p. 76

Caramel Pear Pudding

(Pictured below)

Don't expect this old-fashioned dessert to last long. The delicate pears and irresistible caramel topping make it a winner whenever I serve it. It's nice to have a tempting fall cake that puts the season's best pears to excellent use. —Sharon Mensing
Greenfield, Iowa

        1 cup all-purpose flour
        2/3 cup sugar
    1-1/2 teaspoons baking powder
        1/2 teaspoon ground cinnamon
        1/4 teaspoon salt
    Pinch ground cloves
        1/2 cup milk
        4 medium pears, peeled and cut
            into 1/2-inch cubes
        1/2 cup chopped pecans
        3/4 cup packed brown sugar
        1/4 cup butter
        3/4 cup boiling water
    Vanilla ice cream *or* whipped cream, optional

In a mixing bowl, combine the first six ingredients; beat in milk until smooth. Stir in pears and pecans. Spoon into an ungreased 2-qt. baking dish.

In another bowl, combine the brown sugar, butter and water and pour over the batter. Bake, uncovered, at 375° for 45-50 minutes. Serve warm with ice cream or whipped cream if desired. **Yield:** 8 servings.

Minty Cocoa Mousse

(Pictured on page 75)

Junior Mints give the refreshing mint taste to this scrumptious silky mousse. It's one of my best desserts because it's a snap to prepare, yet the flavor is beyond compare. —Melissa Tarbox
Allen, Texas

        2 tablespoons baking cocoa
        2 tablespoons milk
        1 cup Junior Mints
        2 tablespoons butter
        1 carton (8 ounces) frozen whipped
            topping, thawed, *divided*
        1/2 teaspoon vanilla extract
    Fresh mint and additional whipped topping,
        optional

In a saucepan, combine cocoa and milk until smooth. Add mints and butter; cook and stir over low heat until smooth. Cool for 15 minutes.

Stir in 1 cup whipped topping and vanilla. Fold in the remaining whipped topping. Spoon into individual dessert dishes. Refrigerate until serving. Garnish with mint and whipped topping if desired. **Yield:** 4 servings.

Rich Chocolate Pudding

Creamy, smooth and fudgy, this dessert is a true chocolate indulgence. With just four ingredients, it might be the easiest from-scratch pudding you'll ever make. —Verna Hainer, Aurora, Colorado

        2 cups (12 ounces) semisweet chocolate
            chips
        1/3 cup confectioners' sugar
        1 cup milk
        1/4 cup butter
    Whipped topping and miniature semisweet
        chocolate chips, optional

Place chips and confectioners' sugar in a blender; cover and process until chips are coarsely chopped. In a saucepan over medium heat, bring milk and butter to a boil. Add to blender; cover and process until chips are melted and mixture is smooth.

Pour into six individual serving dishes. Refrigerate. Garnish with whipped topping and miniature chips if desired. **Yield:** 6 servings.

Apricot Rice Custard

(Pictured above)

Creamy rice custard drizzled with apricot sauce makes a comforting dessert or a refreshingly different breakfast. I haven't been cooking all that long, but it's easy to impress people with this recipe, since it's simple and delicious.
— Elizabeth Montgomery, Taylorville, Illinois

  1 cup uncooked long grain rice
  3 cups milk
1/2 cup sugar
1/2 teaspoon salt
  2 eggs, lightly beaten
1/2 teaspoon vanilla extract
1/4 teaspoon almond extract
Dash ground cinnamon

SAUCE:
  1 can (8-1/2 ounces) apricot halves
  1 can (8 ounces) crushed pineapple, undrained
1/3 cup packed brown sugar
  2 tablespoons lemon juice
  1 tablespoon cornstarch

In a large saucepan, cook rice according to package directions. Stir in milk, sugar and salt; bring to a boil. Reduce heat to low. Stir 1/2 cup into eggs; return all to the pan. Cook and stir for 15 minutes or until mixture coats a spoon (do not boil). Remove from the heat; stir in extracts and cinnamon.

For sauce, drain apricot syrup into a saucepan. Chop apricots; add to syrup. Stir in remaining sauce ingredients; bring to a boil. Boil for 2 minutes, stirring occasionally. Serve sauce and custard warm or chilled. **Yield:** 8-10 servings.

1/2 cup plus 6 teaspoons sugar, *divided*
3 teaspoons vanilla extract

In a saucepan, heat cream over medium-low until almost simmering; remove from the heat. In a mixing bowl, beat egg yolks and 1/2 cup sugar until thick and lemon-colored. Gradually beat in cream; add vanilla. Pour into six ungreased 6-oz. custard cups. Place cups in a 13-in. x 9-in. x 2-in. baking pan. Fill pan with boiling water to a depth of 1 in.

Bake at 350° for 45 minutes or until custard center is almost set. Remove cups from pan to a wire rack; cool for 15 minutes. Refrigerate for at least 2 hours or until chilled. Sprinkle with remaining sugar. Broil 4-6 in. from the heat for 2 minutes or until golden brown. Serve immediately. **Yield:** 6 servings.

Peanut Butter Pudding

For a creamy, comforting dessert, this smooth pudding can't be beat. I hope you try it soon.
— *Edna Hoffman, Hebron, Indiana*

1/3 cup sugar
4-1/2 teaspoons cornstarch
1/4 teaspoon salt
1-1/2 cups milk
1/2 cup half-and-half cream
1/2 cup creamy peanut butter
1 teaspoon vanilla extract
Whipped cream, optional

In a saucepan, combine sugar, cornstarch and salt. Gradually stir in milk and cream; bring to a boil over medium heat. Cook and stir for 2 minutes. Remove from the heat; stir in peanut butter and vanilla until smooth. Pour into serving dishes; refrigerate. Garnish with whipped cream if desired. **Yield:** 4 servings.

Coconut Custard

My family always thought baked custard was a treat...and I especially like this version made with coconut. — *Ruth Peterson, Jenison, Michigan*

4 eggs
1/3 cup sugar
1/2 teaspoon salt
1/2 teaspoon vanilla extract
3 cups milk
1 cup flaked coconut
Dash ground nutmeg
MELBA SAUCE:
5 teaspoons cornstarch

Fruit-Topped Almond Cream

(Pictured above)

This is a light and refreshing dessert. It's delicious with berries, but it can be made all year using whatever fruit is available. — *Donna Friedrich Fishkill, New York*

1 package (3.4 ounces) instant French vanilla pudding mix
2-1/2 cups cold milk
1 cup heavy whipping cream
1/2 to 3/4 teaspoon almond extract
3 cups assorted fruit (strawberries, grapes, raspberries, blueberries, mandarin oranges)

In a large mixing bowl, combine pudding mix and milk. Beat on low speed for 2 minutes; set aside. In a small mixing bowl, beat cream and extract until stiff peaks form. Fold into pudding. Spoon into a shallow 2-qt. serving dish. Chill. Top with fruit just before serving. **Yield:** 8 servings.

Burnt Custard

The recipe for this smooth-as-silk custard came from a local restaurant years ago. With its broiled topping, it looks pretty in individual cups.
— *Heidi Main, Anchorage, Alaska*

2 cups heavy whipping cream
4 egg yolks

        1/3 cup cold water
     2 cups fresh *or* frozen raspberries,
thawed
     2/3 cup sugar
     1/4 teaspoon salt

In a bowl, beat eggs. Add sugar, salt and vanilla. Gradually add milk; mix well. Stir in coconut. Place six ungreased 10-oz. ramekins or custard cups in a 13-in. x 9-in. x 2-in. baking dish. Fill each with about 3/4 cup coconut mixture. Sprinkle with nutmeg.

Fill larger pan with boiling water to a depth of 1 in. Bake at 325° for 30-40 minutes or until center is just set (mixture will jiggle). Remove ramekins from pan to a wire rack.

In a saucepan, combine cornstarch and water until smooth. Add raspberries, sugar and salt. Bring to a boil; cook and stir for 2 minutes or until thickened. Remove from the heat; strain if desired. Cool. Serve over custard. **Yield:** 6 servings.

White Chocolate Mousse

This elegant, fluffy dessert is a feast for the eyes and palate. My family loves it and the recipe is easy to double if you are hosting a larger group.
—Susan Herbert, Aurora, Illinois

     1 cup heavy whipping cream
     2 tablespoons sugar
     1 package (3 ounces) cream cheese,
         softened
     3 squares (1 ounce *each*) white baking
         chocolate, melted
     2 cups blueberries, raspberries *or*
         strawberries
Additional berries, optional

In a mixing bowl, beat cream until soft peaks form. Gradually add sugar, beating until stiff peaks form; set aside. In another mixing bowl, beat cream cheese until fluffy. Add chocolate and beat until smooth. Fold in whipped cream.

Alternate layers of mousse and berries in parfait glasses, ending with mousse. Garnish with additional berries if desired. Serve immediately or refrigerate for up to 3 hours. **Yield:** 4-6 servings.

Pineapple Rice Pudding

(Pictured at right)

An aunt who lived in Hawaii shared the recipe for this tropical-tasting rice pudding. It's my family's favorite comfort food. —Joan Hallford
North Richland Hills, Texas

     4 cups milk, *divided*
     3 cups cooked long grain rice
     2/3 cup sugar
     1/2 teaspoon salt
     1 package (3 ounces) cream cheese,
         softened
     2 eggs
     1 teaspoon vanilla extract
PINEAPPLE SAUCE:
     1 can (20 ounces) pineapple chunks
     1/4 cup packed brown sugar
     1 tablespoon cornstarch
     1 tablespoon butter
     1/8 teaspoon salt
     1/2 teaspoon vanilla extract

In a saucepan, combine 3-1/2 cups milk, rice, sugar and salt; bring to a boil over medium heat. Cook for 15 minutes or until thick and creamy, stirring occasionally. In a mixing bowl, beat the cream cheese. Beat in eggs and remaining milk. Stir into rice mixture.

Cook and stir for 2 minutes over medium heat until mixture reaches 160°. Stir in vanilla. Spoon into six dessert dishes. Drain pineapple, reserving the juice; set the pineapple aside.

In a saucepan, combine brown sugar, cornstarch, butter, salt and reserved pineapple juice. Bring to boil; cook and stir for 2 minutes or until thickened. Stir in vanilla and pineapple. Spoon over pudding. **Yield:** 6 servings.

Berry Cream Dessert

(Pictured below)

When I was in high school, my best friend's mom used to make this light berry dessert...and I fell in love with it! Now I fix it for my family on special occasions. Yogurt gives it a deliciously tangy taste.
—Deb Sandoval
Colorado Springs, Colorado

> **1 package (3 ounces) strawberry gelatin**
> **1 package (3 ounces) raspberry gelatin**
> **2 cups boiling water**
> **2 cups cold water**
> **1 carton (8 ounces) strawberry yogurt**
> **1 carton (8 ounces) raspberry yogurt**
> **2 cups sliced fresh *or* frozen unsweetened strawberries**
> **1 carton (12 ounces) frozen whipped topping, thawed**
> **Additional fresh strawberries, optional**

In a large bowl, dissolve strawberry and raspberry gelatin in boiling water. Stir in cold water and strawberry and raspberry yogurt until blended. Chill until syrupy, about 1 hour.

Fold in strawberries and whipped topping. Spoon into individual dishes. Chill until firm, about 4 hours. Garnish with fresh berries if desired. **Yield:** 16 servings.

Danish Rhubarb Pudding

My family loves this pudding's sweet, delicious, distinctive flavor. Since the pudding is soft-set, it could also be used as a sauce over ice cream or pound cake. —Kay Sundheim, Nashua, Montana

> **6 cups chopped fresh *or* frozen rhubarb, thawed**
> **6 cups water**
> **2 cups sugar**
> **1/4 cup cornstarch**
> **3 tablespoons cold water**

In a saucepan, bring rhubarb and water to a boil. Reduce heat; simmer, uncovered, for 10-15 minutes or until rhubarb is tender. Drain, reserving liquid; discard pulp. Measure 4 cups liquid; return to the pan.

Add sugar; bring to a boil. Combine cornstarch and cold water until smooth; stir into rhubarb liquid. Cook and stir for 1-2 minutes or until slightly thickened. Pour into individual dishes. Refrigerate for at least 4 hours before serving. **Yield:** 8 servings.

Blueberry-Topped Custard

A silky texture, rich vanilla flavor and fruit topping make this lovely dessert extra special.
—DeEtta Rasmussen, Fort Madison, Iowa

> **1/2 cup sugar**
> **2 tablespoons all-purpose flour**
> **1/8 teaspoon salt**
> **1-1/2 cups half-and-half cream**
> **1 teaspoon grated lemon peel**
> **3 egg yolks, lightly beaten**
> **2 tablespoons butter**
> **1 tablespoon vanilla extract**
> **1 can (15 ounces) blueberries**
> **1 tablespoon cornstarch**

In a saucepan, combine the sugar, flour and salt. Gradually add cream and lemon peel until blended. Bring to a boil; cook and stir for 2 minutes or until thickened and bubbly. Remove from the heat.

Stir a small amount of hot mixture into egg yolks. Return all to pan; bring to a gentle boil, stirring constantly. Remove from the heat; stir in butter and vanilla. Pour into four parfait glasses or dessert dishes. Cool.

Drain blueberries, reserving juice. Spoon blue-

berries over custard. In a saucepan, combine cornstarch and blueberry juice until smooth. Bring to a boil over medium heat; cook and stir for 1-2 minutes or until thickened. Spoon over berries. **Yield:** 4 servings.

Coconut Cream Pudding

A golden baked meringue makes the crowning touch to this mouthwatering dessert.
—*Verona Koehlmoos, Pilger, Nebraska*

1-1/4 cups sugar, *divided*
1/4 cup cornstarch
3 cups milk
4 eggs, *separated*
1 cup flaked coconut
1 teaspoon vanilla extract

In a heavy saucepan, combine 3/4 cup sugar and cornstarch; stir in milk. Cook and stir over medium heat until thick and bubbly; cook and stir 2 minutes more. Remove from heat.

Beat egg yolks. Stir 1 cup hot milk mixture into yolks; return to pan. Cook and stir over medium heat until gently boiling; cook and stir 2 minutes more. Remove from the heat; cool to lukewarm. Stir in coconut and vanilla. Pour into an ungreased 8-in. square baking dish.

In a mixing bowl, beat egg whites until soft peaks form. Gradually add remaining sugar, beating until stiff peaks form. Spread over pudding, sealing edges. Bake at 350° for 10-15 minutes. Serve warm. **Yield:** 9 servings.

Pretty Cherry Parfaits

These parfaits are just the treat to try when you want to serve a dessert that's easy and lovely.
—*Bernice Morris, Marshfield, Missouri*

1 can (21 ounces) cherry pie filling
1/4 teaspoon almond extract
1 cup (8 ounces) sour cream
1 cup cold milk
1 package (3.4 ounces) instant vanilla pudding mix
Whipped topping, chopped almonds and fresh mint, optional

Combine pie filling and extract; set aside. In a mixing bowl, combine sour cream and milk. Stir in pudding mix; beat on low speed for 2 minutes.

Spoon half into parfait glasses; top with half of the pie filling. Repeat layers. Garnish with whipped

topping, almonds and mint if desired. Refrigerate until serving. **Yield:** 4-6 servings.

Pumpkin Custard

(Pictured above)

This dessert is a refreshing departure from pumpkin pie, but it has the same old-fashioned flavor.
—*Andrea Holcomb, Torrington, Connecticut*

1 can (15 ounces) solid-pack pumpkin
2 eggs
1 cup half-and-half cream
2/3 cup packed brown sugar
1-1/2 teaspoons pumpkin pie spice
1/2 teaspoon salt
TOPPING:
1/4 cup packed brown sugar
1/4 cup chopped pecans
1 tablespoon butter, melted
Whipped cream and ground cinnamon

In a mixing bowl, combine the first six ingredients; beat until smooth. Pour into four greased 10-oz. custard cups. Place in a 13-in. x 9-in. x 2-in. baking pan; pour hot water around cups to a depth of 1 in. Bake, uncovered, at 350° for 20 minutes.

Meanwhile, in a small bowl, combine the brown sugar, pecans and butter. Sprinkle over custard. Bake 30-35 minutes longer or until a knife inserted near the center comes out clean. Serve warm or chilled; top with whipped cream and cinnamon. **Yield:** 4 servings.

1 cup maple syrup
2 cups milk, *divided*
2 tablespoons cornstarch
1/4 teaspoon salt
2 eggs, lightly beaten
1 cup finely chopped walnuts

In the top of a double boiler over boiling water, heat syrup and 1-3/4 cups milk until bubbles form around sides of pan. Combine cornstarch, salt and remaining milk; gradually add to syrup mixture. Cook and stir until thickened, about 25 minutes. Add a small amount to eggs. Return all to pan; cook for 5 minutes. Pour into serving dishes. Sprinkle with walnuts; cool. **Yield:** 6 servings.

Lemon-Lime Mousse

For a light and refreshing dessert after any meal, try this tangy citrus treat. —Kathryn Anderson
Wallkill, New York

1/2 cup sugar
2 tablespoons cornstarch
Pinch salt
3 egg yolks
2/3 cup milk
1/4 cup lemon juice
1 tablespoon lime juice
1-1/2 teaspoons grated lemon peel
1/2 teaspoon grated lime peel
1 cup heavy whipping cream, whipped
Lime slices and additional lemon peel,
optional

In a saucepan, combine sugar, cornstarch and salt. In a bowl, whisk the egg yolks and milk; stir into sugar mixture. Add juices; whisk until smooth. Cook and stir over medium heat until mixture comes to a boil. Cook and stir 2 minutes longer. Add lemon and lime peel.

Cover surface with plastic wrap; refrigerate until completely cooled. Fold in whipped cream. Spoon into individual dishes. Garnish with lime slices and lemon peel if desired. **Yield:** 6 servings.

Banana Custard Pudding

(Pictured above)

I absolutely love this pudding that is easy to stir up anytime! —Hazel Fritchie, Palestine, Illinois

1/2 cup sugar
1 tablespoon cornstarch
1/8 teaspoon salt
1-1/2 cups milk
3 egg yolks, beaten
1 teaspoon vanilla extract
1 medium firm banana, sliced
Fresh mint, optional

In a saucepan, combine sugar, cornstarch and salt. Gradually add milk; cook and stir over medium heat until mixture comes to a boil. Cook and stir 2 minutes longer. Stir a small amount into the egg yolks; return all to pan. Cook and stir until thickened.

Remove from the heat; stir in vanilla. Chill for 1 hour. Just before serving, fold in banana. Garnish with mint if desired. **Yield:** 4 servings.

Maple Walnut Cream

We vacation often in Vermont and always come home with some real maple syrup. This dessert is a terrific way to use the syrup, all the time reminding us of the wonderful time we had on vacation.
—Ida Hartnett, Sparta, New Jersey

Swedish Cream

This thick creamy dessert is a great finale to a hearty meal. It has a hint of almond flavor and looks spectacular. —Linda Nilsen, Anoka, Minnesota

2 cups heavy whipping cream
1 cup plus 2 teaspoons sugar, *divided*
1 envelope unflavored gelatin
1 teaspoon vanilla extract

1 teaspoon almond extract
2 cups (16 ounces) sour cream
1 cup fresh *or* frozen red raspberries,
  crushed

In a saucepan, combine cream and 1 cup sugar. Cook and stir constantly over low heat until candy thermometer reads 160° or steam rises from pan (do not boil). Stir in gelatin until dissolved; add extracts. Cool 10 minutes. Whisk in sour cream.

Pour into eight dessert glasses or small bowls; chill at least 1 hour. Before serving, combine raspberries and remaining sugar; spoon over each serving. **Yield:** 8 servings.

Blueberry Peach Parfaits

We have peach trees and blueberry bushes, so combining those fresh fruits with a thick old-fashioned custard sauce is an extraordinary treat.
—Suzanne Cleveland, Lyons, Georgia

  1/2 cup sugar
    3 tablespoons cornstarch
  1/4 teaspoon salt
    2 cups milk
    2 eggs, lightly beaten
1-1/2 teaspoons vanilla extract
    2 medium ripe peaches, peeled and sliced
1-1/2 cups fresh blueberries
Whipped cream

In a saucepan, combine the sugar, cornstarch and salt. Stir in milk until smooth. Bring to a boil over medium heat; cook and stir for 2 minutes or until thickened. Remove from the heat. Stir a small amount of hot mixture into eggs; return all to the pan, stirring constantly. Bring to a gentle boil; cook and stir for 2 minutes. Remove from the heat; stir in vanilla. Cover and refrigerate until chilled.

In six parfait glasses, layer 2 rounded tablespoons of custard, two to three peach slices and 2 tablespoons blueberries; repeat layers. Top with whipped cream. **Yield:** 6 servings.

Lemon Bread Pudding

(Pictured at right)

Sweet raisins and a smooth hot lemon sauce make this bread pudding extra special. Even today, I get requests for the recipe from people who tasted this traditional dessert years ago.
—Mildred Sherrer, Bay City, Texas

    3 slices day-old bread, cubed
  3/4 cup raisins

    2 cups milk
  1/2 cup sugar
    2 tablespoons butter
  1/4 teaspoon salt
    2 eggs
    1 teaspoon vanilla extract
LEMON SAUCE:
  3/4 cup sugar
    2 tablespoons cornstarch
    1 cup water
    3 tablespoons lemon juice
    2 teaspoons grated lemon peel
    1 tablespoon butter

Toss bread and raisins in an ungreased 1-1/2-qt. baking dish; set aside. In a saucepan, combine the milk, sugar, butter and salt; cook and stir until the butter melts. Remove from the heat. Whisk eggs and vanilla in a small bowl; gradually stir in a small amount of the hot mixture. Return all to the pan and mix well.

Pour over bread and raisins. Set the dish in a larger baking pan; add 1 in. of hot water. Bake, uncovered, at 350° for 50-60 minutes or until a knife inserted near the center comes out clean.

For sauce, combine the sugar and cornstarch in a saucepan. Stir in water until smooth; bring to a boil over medium heat. Boil for 1-2 minutes, stirring constantly. Remove from the heat; stir in lemon juice, peel and butter until butter melts. Serve over warm or cold pudding. Refrigerate any leftovers. **Yield:** 6 servings.

Rhubarb Gingersnap Parfaits

I created this recipe to showcase one of my favorite garden plants—rhubarb. —Diane Halferty
Corpus Christi, Texas

    4 cups chopped fresh *or* frozen rhubarb
    1/2 cup sugar
    3/4 cup heavy whipping cream
    3 tablespoons confectioners' sugar
    1/3 cup sour cream
    1/8 teaspoon almond extract
    2 tablespoons coarsely crushed
        gingersnaps

In a large saucepan, bring rhubarb and sugar to a boil over medium heat, stirring constantly. Reduce heat; simmer, uncovered, until rhubarb is tender and mixture is reduced to 1-1/3 cups. Remove from heat. Cool for 30 minutes. Cover; refrigerate.

In a mixing bowl, beat the whipping cream until soft peaks form. Beat in confectioners' sugar. Add sour cream and extract; beat until stiff peaks form. In four parfait glasses, place about 2 tablespoons rhubarb mixture and 1/4 cup cream mixture; repeat layers. Sprinkle with gingersnaps. Refrigerate until serving. **Yield:** 4 servings.

Dark Chocolate Pudding

This rich old-fashioned treat is oh-so-creamy and comforting! —Lillian Julow, Gainesville, Florida

    1/4 cup sugar
    3 tablespoons cornstarch
    1/4 teaspoon salt
    2 cups milk
    3 egg yolks, beaten
    1 dark chocolate candy bar (7 ounces),
        melted
    1/2 teaspoon vanilla extract
Whipped cream, grated chocolate and
    Pirouette cookies

In a large saucepan, combine the sugar, cornstarch and salt. Stir in milk until smooth. Cook and stir over medium-high heat until thickened and bubbly. Reduce heat; cook and stir 2 minutes longer. Remove from the heat.

Stir a small amount of hot mixture into egg yolks; return all to pan, stirring constantly. Bring to a gentle boil; cook and stir 2 minutes longer. Remove from the heat; gradually whisk in chocolate and vanilla until smooth.

Press plastic wrap onto surface of pudding. Refrigerate. Spoon into dessert dishes. Garnish with whipped cream, grated chocolate and cookies.

Serve warm or cold. **Yield:** 4-6 servings.

Editor's Note: This recipe was tested with Hershey's Special Dark chocolate and Pepperidge Farm Pirouette cookies.

Berry Cheesecake Parfaits

I can serve up this easy dessert in no time. Impressive and delicious, it's just right after a full meal. —Joyce Mart, Wichita, Kansas

    1 package (8 ounces) cream cheese,
        softened
    2 to 4 tablespoons sugar
    1/2 cup vanilla yogurt
    2 cups fresh raspberries *or* berries of
        your choice
    1/2 cup graham cracker crumbs (8 squares)

In a mixing bowl, beat cream cheese and sugar until smooth. Stir in yogurt. In parfait glasses or bowls, alternate layers of berries, cream cheese mixture and cracker crumbs. Serve immediately or refrigerate for up to 8 hours. **Yield:** 4 servings.

Cherry Bavarian Cream

I like recipes for out-of-the-ordinary treats. This is a not-too-sweet dessert that's worth the extra effort. —Christina Till, South Haven, Michigan

    6 egg yolks
    1/2 cup sugar
    2 cups warm milk (115° to 120°)
    1 tablespoon vanilla extract
    2 envelopes unflavored gelatin
    1/4 cup cold water
    1 cup heavy whipping cream, whipped
    2 cups pitted tart red *or* bing cherries
Red food coloring, optional
Fresh mint, optional

In the top of a double boiler, beat egg yolks and sugar with an electric mixer for 2 minutes. Gradually add milk and vanilla. Place over boiling water. Cook and stir constantly for 6-8 minutes or until mixture begins to coat the spoon. Pour into a large bowl; set aside.

Sprinkle gelatin over water; let stand 2 minutes. Stir into egg mixture; tint with food coloring if desired. Set bowl over larger bowl filled with ice water. As soon as cooked mixture begins to set up, fold in cream and cherries. Pour into a 2-qt. serving bowl and refrigerate 4-6 hours or overnight. Garnish with mint if desired. **Yield:** 6-8 servings.

Cream Puffs
& Eclairs

Heart's Delight Eclair, p. 86

Graham Cream Puffs

(Pictured below)

For an exquisite treat, try these "berry" special graham cracker puffs filled with fresh raspberries and cream. —Iola Egle, McCook, Nebraska

    1 cup water
  1/2 cup butter
  1/2 cup all-purpose flour
  1/2 cup graham cracker crumbs
  1/4 teaspoon salt
    4 eggs
GLAZE:
  1/2 cup raspberries
    2 tablespoons sugar
    1 teaspoon cornstarch
  1/2 cup orange juice
FILLING:
    1 cup heavy whipping cream
    1 to 3 tablespoons sugar
    1 teaspoon vanilla extract
    2 cups raspberries, drained

In a saucepan over medium heat, bring water and butter to a boil. Add flour, crumbs and salt all at once; stir until a smooth ball forms. Remove from the heat; let stand for 5 minutes. Add eggs, one at a time, beating well after each. Beat until smooth.

Cover baking sheets with foil; grease foil. Drop batter by 1/4 cupfuls 3 in. apart onto foil. Bake at 400° for 30-35 minutes or until golden brown.

Meanwhile, for glaze, puree berries in a blender; strain and discard seeds. Set the puree aside. Remove puffs to wire racks; immediately cut a slit in each for steam to escape.

In a saucepan, combine sugar and cornstarch; stir in orange juice and the reserved puree. Bring to a boil over medium heat, stirring constantly; boil for 1 minute. Remove from heat; set aside.

In a mixing bowl, beat cream until soft peaks form. Beat in sugar and vanilla. Fold in raspberries. Just before serving, split puffs and remove soft dough. Add filling; replace tops. Drizzle with glaze. **Yield:** 10 servings.

Heart's Delight Eclair

(Pictured on page 85)

This lovely and luscious treat is rumored to have been the favorite dessert of European royalty long ago. I know that it's won the hearts of everyone I've ever made it for. Enjoy! —Lorene Milligan Chemainus, British Columbia

    1 package (17-1/4 ounces) frozen puff pastry, thawed
    3 cups cold milk
    1 package (5.1 ounces) instant vanilla pudding mix
    2 cups heavy whipping cream
    1 teaspoon vanilla extract, *divided*
    1 cup confectioners' sugar
    1 tablespoon water
  1/4 teaspoon almond extract
  1/2 cup semisweet chocolate chips
    1 teaspoon shortening

On a lightly floured surface, roll each puff pastry sheet into a 12-in. square. Using an 11-in. heart pattern, cut each pastry into a heart shape. Place on greased baking sheets. Bake at 400° for 12-15 minutes or until golden brown. Remove to wire racks to cool.

Meanwhile, combine milk and pudding mix until thickened. In a mixing bowl, beat cream and 1/2 teaspoon of vanilla until stiff peaks form. Carefully fold into pudding. Split puff pastry hearts in half. Place one layer on a serving plate. Top with a third of the pudding mixture. Repeat twice. Top with remaining pastry.

In a bowl, combine confectioners' sugar, water, almond extract and the remaining vanilla until smooth. Spread over top. Melt chocolate chips and shortening; pipe in diagonal lines in one direction over frosting. Beginning 1 in. from side of heart, use a sharp knife to draw right angles across the piped lines. Refrigerate until set. **Yield:** 10-12 servings.

State Fair Cream Puffs

The Wisconsin Bakers Association has served these treats at our state fair since 1924. Now I can bake them in my own kitchen! —Ruth Jungbluth Dodgeville, Wisconsin

   1 cup water
1/2 cup butter
   1 cup all-purpose flour
1/4 teaspoon salt
   4 eggs
   2 tablespoons milk
   1 egg yolk, lightly beaten
   2 cups heavy whipping cream
1/4 cup confectioners' sugar
1/2 teaspoon vanilla extract
Additional confectioners' sugar

In a saucepan over medium heat, bring water and butter to a boil. Add flour and salt all at once; stir until a smooth ball forms. Remove from the heat; let stand for 5 minutes. Add eggs, one at a time, beating well after each addition. Beat until smooth.

Drop by 1/4 cupfuls 3 in. apart onto greased baking sheets. Combine milk and egg yolk; brush over puffs. Bake at 400° for 35 minutes or until golden brown. Remove to wire racks. Immediately cut a slit in each for steam to escape; cool.

In a mixing bowl, whip cream until soft peaks form. Gradually add sugar and vanilla, beating until almost stiff. Split puffs; remove soft dough. Add filling; replace tops. Dust with confectioners' sugar. Refrigerate until serving. **Yield:** 10 servings.

Traditional Eclairs

(Pictured above right)

Our Test Kitchen baked puffed pastries to a beautiful golden brown, then filled them with creamy vanilla pudding and frosted them with chocolaty icing for this recipe.

   1 cup water
1/2 cup butter
   1 teaspoon sugar
1/4 teaspoon salt
   1 cup all-purpose flour
   4 eggs
FILLING:
1/3 cup sugar
   3 tablespoons cornstarch
2-1/2 cups milk
   2 egg yolks
   1 tablespoon butter
1-1/2 teaspoons vanilla extract
Confectioners' sugar *or* chocolate frosting

In a saucepan over medium heat, bring water, butter, sugar and salt to a boil. Add flour all at once; stir until a smooth ball forms. Remove from the heat; let stand for 5 minutes. Add eggs, one at a time, beating well with a wooden spoon after each addition. Beat until smooth.

Cut a 1/2-in. hole in the corner of a heavy-duty plastic bag; add batter. Pipe into 12 strips (about 3 in. long) 3 in. apart on a greased baking sheet. Bake at 400° for 30-35 minutes or until golden brown. Remove to a wire rack. Immediately cut a slit in each for steam to escape; cool.

In a saucepan, combine the sugar and cornstarch; gradually add milk until smooth. Cook and stir over medium-high heat until thickened and bubbly. Reduce heat; cook and stir 2 minutes longer. Remove from the heat. Stir 1 cup hot filling into egg yolks; return all to pan. Bring to a gentle boil; cook for 2 minutes, stirring constantly. Remove from the heat; stir in butter and vanilla. Cool.

Split puffs; remove and discard soft dough from inside. Spoon filling into puffs. Replace tops; dust with confectioners' sugar or spread with frosting. Refrigerate until serving. **Yield:** 1 dozen.

Whipping Cream

Cream will whip faster if you chill the beaters and bowl in the freezer for 15 minutes. The cream should also be as cold as possible.

The bowl in which you whip cream should be deep enough so the cream can easily double in volume.

Chocolate-Filled Cream Puffs

(Pictured above)

This is a heavenly dessert for chocolate lovers. Each puff is stuffed with chocolate cream and drizzled with chocolate glaze. —Kathy Kittell
Lenexa, Kansas

   1 cup water
   6 tablespoons butter
   1 cup all-purpose flour
  1/4 teaspoon salt
   4 eggs
FILLING:
   1 cup heavy whipping cream
  1/2 cup confectioners' sugar
   2 tablespoons baking cocoa
GLAZE:
   1 square (1 ounce) unsweetened
     chocolate
   1 tablespoon butter
  1/2 cup confectioners' sugar
   2 tablespoons water

In a saucepan over medium heat, bring water and butter to a boil. Add flour and salt all at once; stir until a smooth ball forms. Remove from the heat; let stand 5 minutes. Add eggs, one at a time, beating well after each addition. Beat until smooth.

Cover a baking sheet with foil; grease foil. Drop batter into six mounds onto foil. Bake at 400° for 15 minutes. Reduce heat to 350°; bake 30 minutes longer. Remove puffs to a wire rack. Immediately cut a slit in each for steam to escape.

In a mixing bowl, beat cream until soft peaks form. Gradually add sugar and cocoa, beating until almost stiff. Split puffs and remove soft dough. Add filling; replace tops. Melt chocolate and butter; stir in sugar and water. Drizzle over puffs. Chill. **Yield:** 6 servings.

Cream Puff Dessert

I recently took this rich dessert to a fellowship meeting at our church. Everyone loved it!
—Lisa Nash, Blaine, Minnesota

1 cup water
1/2 cup butter
1 cup all-purpose flour
4 eggs
FILLING:
1 package (8 ounces) cream cheese,
    softened
3-1/2 cups cold milk
2 packages (3.9 ounces *each*) instant
    chocolate pudding mix
TOPPING:
1 carton (8 ounces) frozen whipped
    topping, thawed
1/4 cup milk chocolate ice cream topping
1/4 cup caramel ice cream topping
1/3 cup chopped almonds

In a saucepan over medium heat, bring water and butter to a boil. Add flour all at once; stir until a smooth ball forms. Remove from the heat; let stand for 5 minutes. Add the eggs, one at a time, beating well after each addition. Beat until smooth.

Spread mixture into a greased 13-in. x 9-in. x 2-in. baking dish. Bake at 400° for 30-35 minutes or until puffed and golden brown. Cool completely on a wire rack.

Meanwhile, in a mixing bowl, beat the cream cheese, milk and pudding mix until smooth. Spread over puff; refrigerate for 20 minutes. Spread with whipped topping; refrigerate until serving. Drizzle with chocolate and caramel toppings; sprinkle with almonds. Store any leftover dessert in the refrigerator. **Yield:** 12 servings.

Chocolate Eclairs

(Pictured at right)

With creamy filling and fudgy frosting, these eclairs are extra special. People are thrilled when these finger-licking-good treats appear on the dessert table.
—Jessica Campbell, Viola, Wisconsin

1 cup water
1/2 cup butter
1 cup all-purpose flour
1/4 teaspoon salt
4 eggs
FILLING:
1 package (5.1 ounces) instant vanilla
    pudding mix
2-1/2 cups cold milk
1 cup heavy whipping cream
1/4 cup confectioners' sugar
1 teaspoon vanilla extract
FROSTING:
2 squares (1 ounce *each*) semisweet
    chocolate

2 tablespoons butter
1-1/4 cups confectioners' sugar
2 to 3 tablespoons hot water

In a saucepan, bring water and butter to a boil. Add the flour and salt all at once. Stir until a smooth ball forms. Remove from the heat; let stand for 5 minutes. Add eggs, one at a time, beating well after each addition until batter becomes smooth.

Using a tablespoon or a pastry tube with a No. 10 or large tip, form dough into 4-in. x 1-1/2-in. strips on a greased baking sheet. Bake at 400° for 35-40 minutes or until puffed and golden. Immediately cut a slit in each to allow steam to escape. Cool on a wire rack.

In a mixing bowl, beat pudding mix and milk according to package directions. In another mixing bowl, whip the cream until soft peaks form. Beat in sugar and vanilla; fold into pudding. Split eclairs; remove soft dough from inside. Fill eclairs (chill any remaining filling for another use).

For frosting, melt chocolate and butter in a saucepan over low heat. Stir in sugar and enough hot water to achieve a smooth consistency. Cool slightly. Frost eclairs. Store in the refrigerator. **Yield:** 9 servings.

Danish Puff

I remember Mom making this cream puff variation for special occasions. Now I make it myself as a treat for friends and family. —Susan Garoutte
Georgetown, Texas

1/2 cup butter
1 cup all-purpose flour
1 to 2 tablespoons cold water
FILLING:
1 cup water
1/2 cup butter
1 cup all-purpose flour
1/4 teaspoon salt
3 eggs
1/2 teaspoon almond extract
TOPPING:
1-1/2 cups confectioners' sugar
2 tablespoons butter, softened
1 to 2 tablespoons water
1-1/2 teaspoons vanilla extract
1/2 cup sliced almonds, toasted

In a bowl, cut the butter into the flour until mixture is crumbly. Sprinkle with water and toss with a fork until moist enough to shape into a ball. Divide in half. On a floured surface, roll each portion into a 12-in. x 3-in. rectangle. Place on greased baking sheets.

In a saucepan, bring water and butter to a boil. Add flour and salt all at once; stir until a smooth ball forms. Remove from the heat; let stand 5 minutes. Add eggs, one at a time, beating well after each. Add extract; beat until smooth. Spread over dough. Bake at 350° for 1 hour or until puffed and golden brown. Cool on pans for 10 minutes.

Combine sugar, butter, water and vanilla until smooth; spread over warm puffs. Sprinkle with almonds. Refrigerate leftovers. **Yield:** 16 servings.

Banana Split Cream Puffs

These fruity cream puff "sandwiches" are a treat that our family has always found scrumptious. For a nice variation, use whipped cream instead of the ice cream called for. —Sandra McKenzie
Braham, Minnesota

1 cup water
1/2 cup butter
1 cup all-purpose flour
1/4 teaspoon salt
4 eggs
12 scoops vanilla ice cream
1 cup sliced fresh strawberries

1 large *or* 2 medium bananas, thinly sliced
1 can (8 ounces) pineapple tidbits, drained
1/2 cup hot fudge sauce

In a saucepan over medium heat, bring water and butter to a boil. Add flour and salt all at once; stir until a smooth ball forms. Remove from the heat; let stand 5 minutes. Add eggs, one at a time, beating well after each addition. Beat until mixture is smooth and shiny, about 3 minutes.

Drop by rounded tablespoonfuls onto a greased baking sheet. Bake at 400° for 30-35 minutes or until golden brown. Transfer to a wire rack. Immediately split puffs open; remove tops and set aside. Discard soft dough from inside. Cool puffs.

Fill each with a scoop of ice cream and top with fruit. Drizzle with hot fudge sauce. Replace tops and serve immediately. **Yield:** 12 servings.

Eclair Torte

Over the years, family, friends, co-workers and students have enjoyed this tried-and-true dessert. For birthdays, our sons prefer it over birthday cake! —Kathy Shepard, Shepherd, Michigan

1 cup water
1/2 cup butter
1/4 teaspoon salt
1 cup all-purpose flour
4 eggs
1 package (8 ounces) cream cheese, softened
2 packages (3.4 ounces *each*) instant vanilla pudding mix
3 cups cold milk
1 carton (12 ounces) frozen whipped topping, thawed
Chocolate syrup

In a saucepan over medium heat, bring water, butter and salt to a boil. Add flour all at once; stir until a smooth ball forms. Remove from the heat; let stand for 5 minutes. Add eggs, one at a time, beating well with a wooden spoon after each addition. Beat until smooth. Spread into a greased 13-in. x 9-in. x 2-in. baking pan.

Bake at 400° for 30-35 minutes or until puffed and golden brown. Cool completely on a wire rack. If desired, remove puff from pan and place on a serving platter.

In a mixing bowl, beat the cream cheese, pudding mix and milk until smooth. Spread over the top of the puff; refrigerate for 20 minutes. Spread with whipped topping; refrigerate. Drizzle with chocolate syrup just before serving. Refrigerate leftovers. **Yield:** 12 servings.

Refrigerator
& Freezer
Desserts

Raspberry Delight, p. 94

Chocolate Peanut Delight

(Pictured below)

A brownie-like crust is packed with nuts, topped with a fluffy peanut butter layer and covered with whipped topping and more nuts. —Karen Kutruff
New Berlin, Pennsylvania

    1 package (18-1/4 ounces) chocolate cake mix
  1/2 cup butter, melted
  1/4 cup milk
    1 egg
    1 cup chopped peanuts, *divided*
    1 package (8 ounces) cream cheese, softened
    1 cup peanut butter
    1 cup confectioners' sugar
    1 can (14 ounces) sweetened condensed milk
1-1/2 teaspoons vanilla extract
    1 carton (16 ounces) frozen whipped topping, thawed, *divided*
  1/2 cup semisweet chocolate chips
4-1/2 teaspoons butter
  1/2 teaspoon vanilla extract

In a mixing bowl, combine dry cake mix, butter, milk and egg. Add 3/4 cup of peanuts. Spread into a greased 13-in. x 9-in. x 2-in. baking pan. Bake at 350° for 30 minutes or until a toothpick inserted near the center comes out clean. Cool on a wire rack.

In a mixing bowl, beat the cream cheese, peanut butter, sugar, condensed milk and vanilla until smooth. Fold in 3 cups whipped topping. Spread over the crust; top with the remaining whipped topping and peanuts.

In a microwave-safe bowl, heat chocolate chips and butter on high for 1 minute or until melted. Stir in vanilla until smooth; drizzle over cake. Refrigerate 2-3 hours before cutting. **Yield:** 12-15 servings.

Cranberry Graham Squares

This pretty dessert is refreshingly creamy and delicious. —H. Stevenson, Davidson, Saskatchewan

    2 cups graham cracker crumbs
    2 tablespoons plus 3/4 cup sugar, *divided*
  1/8 teaspoon salt
  1/2 cup plus 1 tablespoon butter, melted, *divided*
    1 package (3 ounces) cook-and-serve vanilla pudding mix
1-1/2 cups cranberries
  3/4 cup raisins
  3/4 cup water
    2 teaspoons cornstarch
1-1/2 teaspoons cold water
    1 envelope whipped topping mix

In a bowl, combine cracker crumbs, 2 tablespoons sugar, salt and 1/2 cup butter; reserve 1/2 cup. Press the remaining crumbs into an ungreased 9-in. square baking pan. Chill. Meanwhile, cook pudding according to package directions; cool for 5 minutes. Spread over crust. Chill.

In a saucepan over medium heat, cook cranberries, raisins and water until berries pop, about 5-10 minutes. Stir in remaining sugar. Combine cornstarch and cold water until smooth; add to cranberry mixture. Bring to a boil; cook and stir 2 minutes. Remove from heat; stir in remaining butter. Cool to room temperature. Spread over pudding.

Prepare whipped topping according to package directions; spread over cranberry layer. Sprinkle with reserved crumbs. Chill for at least 6 hours. Store in the refrigerator. **Yield:** 9 servings.

Pretzel Dessert

The recipe makes a big batch of this sweet and salty, creamy and crunchy treat.
—Rita Winterberger, Huson, Montana

    2 cups crushed pretzels
  3/4 cup sugar
  3/4 cup butter, melted
    2 envelopes whipped topping mix
    1 cup cold milk
    1 teaspoon vanilla extract
    1 package (8 ounces) cream cheese, cubed

1 cup confectioners' sugar
1 can (21 ounces) cherry pie filling

In a bowl, combine pretzels, sugar and butter; set aside 1/2 cup for topping. Press the remaining mixture into an ungreased 13-in. x 9-in. x 2-in. dish.

In a mixing bowl, beat whipped topping mix, milk and vanilla on high speed for 4 minutes or until soft peaks form. Add cream cheese and confectioners' sugar; beat until smooth. Spread half over crust. Top with the pie filling and remaining cream cheese mixture. Sprinkle with reserved pretzel mixture. Refrigerate overnight. **Yield:** 16 servings.

Orange Charlotte

(Pictured above)

Mom prepared this light and fluffy citrus dessert whenever Dad grilled outdoors. It gave our meals a fresh-tasting finish! —Sue Gronholz
Columbus, Wisconsin

3 envelopes unflavored gelatin
3/4 cup cold water
3/4 cup boiling water
1-1/2 cups orange juice
2 tablespoons lemon juice
1-1/2 teaspoons grated orange peel
1-1/2 cups sugar, *divided*
2-1/2 cups heavy whipping cream
1/2 cup mandarin oranges
3 maraschino cherries

In a large bowl, combine gelatin and cold water; let stand for 10 minutes. Add boiling water; stir until gelatin dissolves. Add juices, orange peel and 3/4 cup sugar. Set bowl in ice water until mixture is syrupy, stirring occasionally. Meanwhile, whip cream until soft peaks form. Gradually add remaining sugar and beat until stiff peaks form. When gelatin mixture begins to thicken, fold in whipped cream.

Lightly coat a 9-in. springform pan with nonstick cooking spray. Pour mixture into pan; chill overnight. Just before serving, run a knife around edge of pan to loosen. Remove sides of pan. Garnish with oranges and cherries. **Yield:** 10-12 servings.

In a small saucepan, combine sugar and corn-starch; gradually stir in water until smooth. Bring to a boil; cook and stir for 1 minute or until thick-ened. Remove from the heat. Stir a small amount of hot filling into egg yolks; return all to the pan, stirring constantly. Bring to a gentle boil; cook and stir for 1 minute. Remove from the heat; stir in butter and lemon peel. Gently stir in lemon juice. Refrig-erate until cool.

In a bowl, combine flour and nuts. Cut in butter until mixture resembles coarse crumbs. Press on-to the bottom of a greased 13-in. x 9-in. x 2-in. baking dish. Bake at 350° for 15-20 minutes or un-til edges are golden brown. Cool on a wire rack.

In a mixing bowl, beat cream cheese and con-fectioners' sugar until smooth; carefully spread over crust. Spread with cooled lemon mixture. In anoth-er mixing bowl, beat milk and pudding mixes on low for 2 minutes; beat in vanilla. Fold in half of the whipped topping. Spread over lemon layer. Spread with remaining whipped topping. Chill for at least 4 hours before cutting. **Yield:** 18-24 servings.

Lemon Cream Dessert

(Pictured above)

My friend Mary and I concocted this easy yet yum-my layered lemon dessert. Our spouses love it.
—Laurel Adams, Danville, Kentucky

1-1/2 cups sugar
  1/3 cup plus 1 tablespoon cornstarch
1-1/2 cups cold water
  3 egg yolks, lightly beaten
  3 tablespoons butter, cubed
  2 teaspoons grated lemon peel
  1/2 cup lemon juice
CRUST:
  1 cup all-purpose flour
  1 cup finely chopped walnuts
  1/2 cup cold butter
TOPPING:
  1 package (8 ounces) cream cheese,
    softened
  1 cup confectioners' sugar
  2 cups cold milk
  2 packages (3.4 ounces *each*) instant
    vanilla pudding mix
  1 teaspoon vanilla extract
  1 carton (16 ounces) frozen whipped
    topping, thawed

Raspberry Delight

(Pictured on page 91)

I knew this cool, fruity and creamy dessert was a winner the first time I tasted it. I confirmed that fact a few summers ago when I entered the recipe in a contest at work—it won first place. —Mary Olson
Albany, Oregon

2-1/4 cups all-purpose flour
  2 tablespoons sugar
  3/4 cup butter, softened
FILLING:
  1 package (8 ounces) cream cheese,
    softened
  1 cup confectioners' sugar
  1 teaspoon vanilla extract
  1/4 teaspoon salt
  2 cups whipped topping
TOPPING:
  1 package (6 ounces) raspberry gelatin
  2 cups boiling water
  2 packages (10 ounces *each*) sweetened
    frozen raspberries
Additional whipped topping and fresh mint,
  optional

In a bowl, combine flour and sugar; blend in butter with a wooden spoon until smooth. Press into an ungreased 13-in. x 9-in. x 2-in. baking pan. Bake at 300° for 20-25 minutes or until set (crust will not brown). Cool. In a mixing bowl, beat cream cheese, confectioners' sugar, vanilla and salt until smooth. Fold in whipped topping. Spread over crust.

For topping, dissolve gelatin in boiling water; stir in raspberries. Chill for 20 minutes or until mixture begins to thicken. Spoon over filling. Refrigerate until set. Cut into squares; garnish with whipped topping and mint if desired. **Yield:** 12-16 servings.

Ice Cream Sundae Dessert

We kids couldn't wait to dig into this tempting ice cream dessert. It's cool and smooth with a ribbon of fudge inside. —Anne Heinonen
Howell, Michigan

2 cups (12 ounces) semisweet chocolate chips
1 can (12 ounces) evaporated milk
1/2 teaspoon salt
1 package (12 ounces) vanilla wafers, crushed
1/2 cup butter, melted
2 quarts vanilla ice cream *or* flavor of your choice, softened

In a saucepan over medium heat, melt chocolate chips with milk and salt; cook and stir until thickened, about 25 minutes. Remove from heat; set aside.

Combine wafer crumbs and butter; set aside 1 cup. Press remaining crumbs into a greased 13-in. x 9-in. x 2-in. pan. Chill for 10-15 minutes. Pour chocolate over crumbs. Cover and freeze for 20-25 minutes or until firm.

Spread the ice cream over chocolate. Sprinkle with reserved crumbs. Freeze at least 2 hours before serving. **Yield:** 12-16 servings.

Pistachio Cookie Dessert

With its smooth pistachio filling, this cool treat is a favorite refreshment at summer 4-H meetings. It's best made and frozen a day in advance. It will thaw as you head to a picnic or potluck.
—Audrey Phillips, Gambier, Ohio

1 quart vanilla ice cream
1 package (20 ounces) chocolate cream-filled sandwich cookies
1/2 cup plus 2 tablespoons butter, melted
1-1/2 cups cold milk
2 packages (3.4 ounces *each*) instant pistachio pudding mix
1 carton (16 ounces) frozen whipped topping, thawed

Soften the ice cream while preparing the crust. Place the cookies in a food processor or blender;

cover and process until fine crumbs form. Stir in the butter. Set aside 1 cup for topping. Press remaining crumb mixture into an ungreased 13-in. x 9-in. x 2-in. dish.

In a mixing bowl, beat milk and pudding mix on low speed for 2 minutes. Gradually add ice cream; mix well. Fold in whipped topping. Spread over crust. Sprinkle reserved crumb mixture over top, pressing down lightly. Cover and freeze for 4 hours or overnight. Remove from the freezer 20 minutes before cutting. **Yield:** 12-15 servings.

Layered Pudding Dessert

(Pictured below)

High on our list of longtime favorites, this fluffy, fruity refrigerated treat continues to hold its own against new dessert recipes I try. —Pat Habiger
Spearville, Kansas

1 cup crushed vanilla wafers, *divided*
1 package (3 ounces) cook-and-serve vanilla pudding mix
2 medium ripe bananas, *divided*
1 package (3 ounces) strawberry gelatin
1 cup whipped topping

Spread half of crushed wafers in bottom of a greased 8-in. square pan. Prepare pudding mix according to package directions; spoon hot pudding over crumbs. Slice one banana; place over pudding. Top with remaining crumbs. Chill 1 hour.

Meanwhile, prepare gelatin according to package directions; chill for 30 minutes or until partially set. Pour over crumbs. Slice the remaining banana and place over gelatin. Spread whipped topping over all. Chill for 2 hours. **Yield:** 9 servings.

Chocolate Cream Dessert

(Pictured below)

Since the 1960s, whenever I've asked my family what dessert I should fix, this is what they've requested. It has a light texture and also a tempting pale chocolate color and is not overly sweet. It's a delightful treat.
—Laurine Muhle
Lake Park, Minnesota

　　3 cups crushed vanilla wafers
　2/3 cup butter, melted
　1/4 cup sugar
　1/2 teaspoon ground cinnamon
FILLING:
　　1 milk chocolate candy bar (7 ounces),
　　　plain *or* with almonds, broken into
　　　pieces
　　1 package (10 ounces) large
　　　marshmallows
　　1 cup milk
　　2 cups heavy whipping cream, whipped
　1/2 teaspoon vanilla extract
Sliced almonds, toasted, optional

In a bowl, combine the vanilla wafer crumbs, butter, sugar and cinnamon and mix well. Set aside 1/3 cup for topping. Press the remaining crumb mixture into a greased 13-in. x 9-in. x 2-in. pan and refrigerate until firm.

In a saucepan, heat candy bar, marshmallows and milk over medium-low heat until chocolate and marshmallows are melted, stirring often.

Remove from the heat and cool to room temperature. Fold in the whipped cream and vanilla; pour over crust. Chill for 3-4 hours. Sprinkle with the reserved crumb mixture and almonds if desired. **Yield:** 12-16 servings.

Gelatin Torte

You can make this lovely summer dessert ahead. The fluffy cake layer is topped with a fruity gelatin mixture. —Sophie Hilicki, Racine, Wisconsin

　　3 eggs, *separated*
　　1 cup sugar, *divided*
　　1 can (8 ounces) crushed pineapple,
　　　drained
　　1 cup graham cracker crumbs
　1/2 teaspoon baking powder
　1/4 cup chopped pecans
　　1 package (6 ounces) cherry gelatin
　　2 cups boiling water
1-1/2 cups cold water
　　3 medium firm bananas, sliced
　　1 cup heavy whipping cream
　　3 tablespoons confectioners' sugar
Maraschino cherries, optional

In a mixing bowl, beat egg yolks and 1/2 cup sugar until thick and lemon-colored. Stir in the pineapple. Combine cracker crumbs and baking powder; stir into the pineapple mixture. Add pecans and set aside. In a mixing bowl, beat egg whites until foamy. Gradually beat in remaining sugar until soft peaks form. Fold into the pineapple mixture. Pour into an ungreased 9-in. springform pan.

Bake at 350° for 30 minutes or until top springs back when lightly touched. Cool on a wire rack. (Do not remove sides of pan.)

Dissolve gelatin in boiling water. Stir in cold water; refrigerate until mixture begins to thicken, about 40 minutes. Stir in bananas; pour over cooled cake layer. Refrigerate until firm, about 2 hours.

In a mixing bowl, beat cream and confectioners' sugar until soft peaks form; pipe or spoon over gelatin layer. Just before serving, run a knife around the edge of pan to loosen; remove sides of pan. Garnish with cherries if desired. **Yield:** 8 servings.

Broken Glass Dessert

When it's cut, this dessert looks like stained glass windows. That's how this recipe got its name!
—Kathy Crow, Cordova, Alaska

　　1 envelope unflavored gelatin
　1/4 cup cold water
　　1 cup pineapple juice

1-1/2 cups graham cracker crumbs
 1/2 cup sugar
 1/2 cup butter, melted
   1 package (3 ounces) lime gelatin
   1 package (3 ounces) strawberry gelatin
   1 package (3 ounces) orange gelatin
4-1/2 cups boiling water, *divided*
   1 carton (8 ounces) frozen whipped
     topping, thawed

Soften the unflavored gelatin in cold water. Boil pineapple juice; stir into unflavored gelatin. Set aside until slightly thickened. Meanwhile, combine the crumbs, sugar and butter; press onto the bottom of a 13-in. x 9-in. x 2-in. greased pan. Chill.

Combine lime gelatin and 1-1/2 cups boiling water; stir until gelatin is dissolved. Pour into an 8-in. x 4-in. x 2-in. loaf pan coated with nonstick cooking spray; chill until very firm. Repeat for strawberry and orange gelatins.

Place whipped topping in a large bowl; gently fold in pineapple juice mixture. When flavored gelatins are firm, cut into 1-in. cubes; gently fold into whipped topping mixture. Spoon over crust. Chill for at least 2 hours. **Yield:** 12-16 servings.

Coconut Crunch Delight

I tasted this light dessert over 10 years ago at a potluck and got the recipe from my mom's dear friend. This is a terrific way to end a heavy meal.
—Debby Chiorino, Oxnard, California

 1/2 cup butter, melted
   1 cup all-purpose flour
1-1/4 cups flaked coconut
 1/4 cup packed brown sugar
   1 cup slivered almonds
   1 package (3.4 ounces) instant vanilla
     pudding mix
   1 package (3.4 ounces) instant coconut
     cream pudding mix
2-2/3 cups cold milk
   2 cups whipped topping
Fresh strawberries, optional

In a bowl, combine the first five ingredients; press lightly into a greased 13-in. x 9-in. x 2-in. baking pan. Bake at 350° for 25-30 minutes or until golden brown, stirring every 10 minutes to form coarse crumbs. Cool. Divide crumb mixture in half; press half into the same baking pan.

In a mixing bowl, beat pudding mixes and milk. Fold in whipped topping; spoon over the crust. Top with remaining crumb mixture. Cover and refrigerate overnight. Garnish with strawberries if desired. **Yield:** 12-16 servings.

Pecan Pumpkin Dessert

(Pictured above)

I always fix this recipe for Thanksgiving. It was given to me by a friend and I've shared it with many others. —Sue Williams, Mt. Holly, North Carolina

   2 cans (15 ounces *each*) solid-pack
     pumpkin
   1 can (12 ounces) evaporated milk
   1 cup sugar
   3 eggs
   1 teaspoon vanilla extract
   1 package (18-1/4 ounces) yellow cake
     mix
   1 cup butter, melted
1-1/2 cups chopped pecans
FROSTING:
   1 package (8 ounces) cream cheese,
     softened
1-1/2 cups confectioners' sugar
   1 teaspoon vanilla extract
   1 carton (12 ounces) frozen whipped
     topping, thawed

Line a 13-in. x 9-in. x 2-in. baking pan with waxed paper and coat the paper with nonstick cooking spray; set aside. In a mixing bowl, combine pumpkin, milk and sugar. Beat in eggs and vanilla. Pour into prepared pan. Sprinkle with dry cake mix and drizzle with butter. Sprinkle with pecans. Bake at 350° for 1 hour or until golden brown. Cool completely in pan on a wire rack. Invert onto a large serving platter; carefully remove waxed paper.

In a mixing bowl, beat cream cheese, confectioners' sugar and vanilla until smooth. Fold in whipped topping. Frost dessert. Store in the refrigerator. **Yield:** 16 servings.

Rhubarb Pudding Dessert

Of the many recipes I've tried with rhubarb as the main ingredient, this is the one my family thinks is best. We can't wait for spring to arrive.
—Marion Meyer, Eau Claire, Wisconsin

 1 cup graham cracker crumbs
 1/4 cup butter, melted
 2 tablespoons sugar
FILLING:
 1 cup sugar
 3 tablespoons cornstarch
 4 cups chopped fresh *or* frozen rhubarb
 1/2 cup water
 3 drops red food coloring, optional
 1/2 cup heavy whipping cream, whipped
 1-1/2 cups miniature marshmallows
 1 package (3.4 ounces) instant vanilla pudding mix

Combine the crumbs, butter and sugar; set aside 2 tablespoons. Press remaining crumbs into an ungreased 11-in. x 7-in. x 2-in. baking dish. Bake at 350° for 8-10 minutes; cool.

For filling, combine sugar and cornstarch in a saucepan. Add rhubarb and water; bring to a boil. Cook and stir for 2 minutes or until thickened. Stir in food coloring if desired. Spread over the crust; chill.

Combine whipped cream and marshmallows; spread over rhubarb layer. Prepare pudding mix according to package directions for pie filling; spread over marshmallow layer. Sprinkle with reserved crumbs. Cover and refrigerate for 4 hours or overnight. **Yield:** 9-12 servings.

Fluffy Pineapple Torte

(Pictured above)

This fluffy dessert is so good after a hearty meal because even a big slice is as light as a feather.
—Gina Squires, Salem, Oregon

1-1/2 cups graham cracker crumbs
 1/4 cup butter, melted
 2 tablespoons sugar
FILLING:
 1 can (12 ounces) evaporated milk
 1 package (3 ounces) lemon gelatin
 1 cup boiling water
 1 package (8 ounces) cream cheese, softened
 1/2 cup sugar
 1 can (8 ounces) crushed pineapple, drained
 1 cup chopped walnuts, *divided*

Combine crumbs, butter and sugar; press into the bottom of an 11-in. x 7-in. x 2-in. baking dish. Bake at 325° for 10 minutes; cool.

Place can of evaporated milk in the refrigerator for 1-1/2 hours. Meanwhile, in a small bowl, dissolve gelatin in water; chill until syrupy, about 1-1/2 hours. In a small mixing bowl, beat milk until stiff peaks form. In a large mixing bowl, beat cream cheese and sugar until smooth. Add gelatin; mix well. Stir in pineapple and 3/4 cup walnuts. Fold in milk. Pour over crust.

Chill for at least 3 hours or overnight. Sprinkle remaining walnuts over the top before filling is completely firm. **Yield:** 12 servings.

Strawberry Yogurt Crunch

This is a very light and delicious dessert. It's a wonderful dish to top off a spring meal. —Becky Palac, Escondido, California

 3/4 cup butter, softened
 1/3 cup packed brown sugar
 1/2 cup all-purpose flour
 1/2 teaspoon ground cinnamon
 1/4 teaspoon baking soda
 1 cup quick-cooking oats
 1 cup flaked coconut, toasted
 1/3 cup chopped nuts
 1 carton (8 ounces) frozen whipped topping, thawed
 2 cartons (6 ounces *each*) strawberry custard-style yogurt *or* flavor of your choice

In a mixing bowl, cream butter and brown sugar. Combine the flour, cinnamon and baking soda;

gradually add to creamed mixture. Stir in the oats, coconut and nuts. Remove 1 cup for topping. Press remaining oat mixture into an ungreased 13-in. x 9-in. x 2-in. baking dish. Bake at 350° for 12-13 minutes or until light brown. Cool on a wire rack.

In a bowl, fold whipped topping into yogurt. Spread over crust. Sprinkle with reserved oat mixture. Cover and refrigerate for 4 hours or overnight. **Yield:** 12-15 servings.

Frozen Peach Dessert

In this recipe, some simple ingredients—peaches, sugar and cream—combine in a delightful way.
—*Sharon Bickett, Chester, South Carolina*

    2 cups sliced peeled fresh *or* frozen
      peaches
  2/3 cup sugar
    2 cups heavy whipping cream
    3 to 4 drops almond extract
Fresh mint and additional peaches, optional

In a blender or food processor, process peaches until smooth. Transfer to a bowl; add sugar. Let stand for 1 hour. In a mixing bowl, beat cream and extract until soft peaks form. Fold into the peach mixture. Pour into a 6-cup mold or freezer-safe bowl that has been lined with plastic wrap. Cover and freeze overnight.

Unmold onto a serving plate about 1 hour before serving. Return to the freezer. Before serving, garnish with mint and peaches if desired. Cut into wedges. **Yield:** 10 servings.

Triple Sherbet Dessert

For a special, refreshing and lovely treat, try this sherbet dessert. —*Mrs. Howard Hinseth Minneapolis, Minnesota*

    1 package (14-1/2 ounces) coconut
      macaroon cookies, crumbled
    1 carton (12 ounces) frozen whipped
      topping, thawed
  1/2 cup chopped pecans, optional
  1/2 cup flaked coconut
    1 pint *each* orange, lemon and lime
      sherbet, softened

In a bowl, combine the cookie crumbs, whipped topping, pecans and coconut. Spread half into a 13-in. x 9-in. x 2-in. dish. Spread with orange sherbet; freeze for 10-15 minutes. Repeat with lemon and lime layers. Top with the remaining cookie mixture. Cover and freeze until firm. **Yield:** 12-16 servings.

Cherry Cheese Delight

(Pictured below)

You couldn't ask for anything more than a nutty crust topped with a smooth cream cheese mixture and sweet cherries. Since this dessert is made the night before, you don't have to worry about last-minute fuss.
—*Kathy Branch*
West Palm Beach, Florida

    1 cup all-purpose flour
    1 cup chopped pecans
  1/2 cup packed brown sugar
  1/2 cup butter, softened
FILLING:
    2 packages (8 ounces *each*) cream
      cheese, softened
  1/2 cup confectioners' sugar
    1 teaspoon vanilla extract
    1 carton (12 ounces) frozen whipped
      topping, thawed
    2 cans (21 ounces *each*) cherry pie filling

In a bowl, combine flour, pecans and brown sugar. With a fork, stir in butter until crumbly. Lightly pat into an ungreased 13-in. x 9-in. x 2-in. baking dish. Bake at 350° for 18-20 minutes or until golden brown. Cool completely.

For filling, in a mixing bowl, beat the cream cheese, confectioners' sugar and vanilla until smooth. Fold in whipped topping. Carefully spread over crust. Top with pie filling. Cover and refrigerate for at least 2 hours. **Yield:** 12-15 servings.

Rhubarb Meringue Dessert

(Pictured below)

I hear so many nice comments when I serve this special springtime dessert. I make it often when our abundant rhubarb is in its prime. It's just as homey as a rhubarb custard pie, but it easily serves a group. —Jessica Moch, Bismarck, North Dakota

    2 cups all-purpose flour
    2 tablespoons sugar
    1 cup cold butter
FILLING:
    2 cups sugar
    1/3 cup all-purpose flour
    1 teaspoon salt
    6 egg yolks, beaten
    1 cup heavy whipping cream
    5 cups sliced fresh *or* frozen rhubarb,
       thawed
MERINGUE:
    6 egg whites
    1/2 teaspoon cream of tartar
    3/4 cup sugar
    1 teaspoon vanilla extract

In a bowl, combine the flour and sugar; cut in butter until crumbly. Press into a greased 13-in. x 9-in. x 2-in. baking dish. Bake at 350° for 20 minutes. Cool on a wire rack while preparing filling. In a bowl, combine the sugar, flour and salt. Stir in egg yolks and cream. Add rhubarb. Pour over crust. Bake at 350° for 50-60 minutes or until set.

In a mixing bowl, beat egg whites and cream of tartar on medium speed until soft peaks form. Gradually beat in sugar, a tablespoon at a time, until stiff peaks form. Beat in vanilla. Spread over hot filling. Bake for 12-15 minutes or until golden brown. Cool on a wire rack. Refrigerate for 1-2 hours before serving. Refrigerate leftovers. **Yield:** 12-15 servings.

Fluffy Mint Dessert

The cool, minty flavor of this fluffy dessert is perfect for Christmas or the hot summer months. Since it has to be made ahead of time, it's a great time-saver on potluck day. —Carol Mixter, Lincoln Park, Michigan

    1 package (14 ounces) cream-filled
       chocolate sandwich cookies,
       crushed
    1/2 cup butter, melted
    2 cartons (12 ounces *each*) frozen
       whipped topping, thawed
    2 cups pastel miniature marshmallows
 1-1/3 cups small pastel mints (5-1/2 ounces)

Reserve 1/4 cup of crushed cookies for garnish. Combine the remaining cookies with butter; press into an ungreased 13-in. x 9-in. x 2-in. baking dish.
   Fold together whipped topping, marshmallows and mints; pour over crust. Garnish with reserved cookies. Cover and refrigerate for 1-2 days before serving. **Yield:** 18-20 servings.

Banana Split Supreme

This lovely and delightful dessert has the classic flavor of a banana split. It's a cool, creamy treat with no last-minute fuss since you just pull it from the freezer. It always solicits praise from our big family. —Marye Franzen, Gothenburg, Nebraska

    3/4 cup butter, *divided*
    2 cups confectioners' sugar
    1 cup evaporated milk
    3/4 cup semisweet chocolate chips
    24 cream-filled chocolate sandwich
       cookies, crushed
    3 to 4 medium firm bananas, cut
       into 1/2-inch slices
    2 quarts vanilla ice cream, softened,
       divided
    1 can (20 ounces) crushed pineapple,
       drained
    1 jar (10 ounces) maraschino cherries,
       drained and halved

3/4 cup chopped pecans
Whipped topping, optional

In a saucepan, combine 1/2 cup butter, sugar, milk and chocolate chips. Bring to a boil over medium heat; boil and stir for 8 minutes. Remove from the heat and cool completely.

Meanwhile, melt the remaining butter; toss with cookie crumbs. Press into a greased 13-in. x 9-in. x 2-in. pan. Freeze for 15 minutes. Arrange banana slices over crust; spread with 1 quart of ice cream. Top with 1 cup of chocolate sauce. Freeze for 1 hour. Refrigerate remaining chocolate sauce. Spread the remaining ice cream over dessert; top with pineapple, cherries and pecans. Cover and freeze several hours or overnight.

Remove from the freezer 10 minutes before serving. Reheat the chocolate sauce. Cut dessert into squares; serve with chocolate sauce and whipped topping if desired. **Yield:** 12-15 servings.

Frozen Mocha Marbled Loaf

This showstopping marbled dessert seems fancy, but it's really simple to prepare ahead and pop in the freezer. Frosty slices have a creamy blend of chocolate and coffee. —Cheryl Martinetto
Grand Rapids, Minnesota

2 cups finely crushed chocolate cream-filled sandwich cookies (about 22 cookies)
3 tablespoons butter, melted
1 package (8 ounces) cream cheese, softened
1 can (14 ounces) sweetened condensed milk
1 teaspoon vanilla extract
2 cups heavy whipping cream, whipped
2 tablespoons instant coffee granules
1 tablespoon hot water
1/2 cup chocolate syrup

Line a 9-in. x 5-in. x 3-in. loaf pan with foil. In a bowl, combine the cookie crumbs and butter. Press firmly onto the bottom and 1-1/2 in. up the sides of prepared pan.

In a mixing bowl, beat cream cheese until light. Add milk and vanilla; mix well. Fold in whipped cream. Spoon half of the mixture into another bowl and set aside. Dissolve coffee in hot water; fold into remaining cream cheese mixture. Fold in chocolate syrup.

Spoon half of chocolate mixture over crust. Top with half of the reserved cream cheese mixture. Repeat layers. Cut through layers with a knife to swirl the chocolate (pan will be full). Cover and freeze for 6 hours or overnight. To serve, lift out of the pan; remove foil. Cut into slices. **Yield:** 12 servings.

Butterscotch Pecan Dessert

(Pictured above)

Light and creamy, this terrific treat never lasts long when I serve it. The fluffy cream cheese layer topped with cool butterscotch pudding is a lip-smacking combination. —Becky Harrison
Albion, Illinois

1/2 cup cold butter
1 cup all-purpose flour
3/4 cup chopped pecans, *divided*
1 package (8 ounces) cream cheese, softened
1 cup confectioners' sugar
1 carton (8 ounces) frozen whipped topping, thawed, *divided*
3-1/2 cups milk
2 packages (3.4 or 3.5 ounces *each*) instant butterscotch *or* vanilla pudding mix

In a bowl, cut the butter into the flour until crumbly; stir in 1/2 cup pecans. Press into an ungreased 13-in. x 9-in. x 2-in. baking pan. Bake at 350° for 20 minutes or until lightly browned. Cool.

In a mixing bowl, beat cream cheese and sugar until fluffy. Fold in 1 cup whipped topping; spread over crust. Combine milk and pudding mix until smooth; pour over cream cheese layer.

Refrigerate for 15-20 minutes or until set. Top with remaining whipped topping and pecans. Refrigerate for 1-2 hours. **Yield:** 16-20 servings.

Frozen Peanut Butter Torte

When you're entertaining guests or seeking an everyday festive finale, you can't miss with this peanutty summer dessert. —Penney Kester
Springville, New York

 1/2 cup all-purpose flour
 1/3 cup quick-cooking oats
 1/4 cup sugar
 1/4 cup butter, softened
 1/4 teaspoon baking soda
 1/2 cup crunchy peanut butter
 1/3 cup light corn syrup
 2 tablespoons honey
 1/2 gallon vanilla ice cream, softened
 3/4 cup chopped salted peanuts

Combine the first five ingredients; mix well. Pat into a greased 9-in. square baking pan. Bake at 350° for 15-17 minutes or until lightly browned. Cool to room temperature.

Combine the peanut butter, corn syrup and honey; carefully spread half over crust. Spread with half the ice cream. Drop remaining peanut butter mixture over ice cream. Sprinkle with half the nuts. Top with remaining ice cream and nuts. Freeze until firm, 3-4 hours. Let stand 5-10 minutes before serving. **Yield:** 9-12 servings.

Make-Ahead Shortcake

My lovely layered dessert showcases strawberries. This family favorite has all the satisfaction of traditional strawberry shortcake with just a dash of distinction. —Karen Bland, Gove, Kansas

 1 loaf (14 ounces) angel food cake, cut
   into 1-inch slices
 1/2 cup cold milk
 1 package (5.1 ounces) instant vanilla
   pudding mix
 1 pint vanilla ice cream, softened
 1 package (6 ounces) strawberry gelatin
 1 cup boiling water
 2 packages (10 ounces *each*) frozen
   sweetened sliced strawberries
Sliced fresh strawberries, optional

Arrange cake slices in a single layer in an ungreased 13-in. x 9-in. x 2-in. dish. In a mixing bowl, beat milk and pudding mix for 2 minutes or until thickened; beat in ice cream. Pour over cake. Chill. In a bowl, dissolve gelatin in boiling water; stir in frozen strawberries. Chill until partially set. Spoon

over pudding mixture. Chill until firm. Garnish with fresh strawberries if desired. **Yield:** 12 servings.

Toffee Mocha Dessert

Angel food cake takes on richness and bold flavor in this special treat. —Jean Ecos
Waukesha, Wisconsin

 1 angel food cake (8 inches), cut
   into 1-inch cubes
 3/4 cup strong brewed coffee, cooled
 1 package (8 ounces) cream cheese,
   softened
 1/2 cup chocolate syrup
 2 to 4 tablespoons sugar
 2 cups whipped topping
 2 Heath bars (1.4 ounces *each*), crushed
Additional Heath bars, optional

Place cake cubes in an ungreased 13-in. x 9-in. x 2-in. dish. Add coffee and toss lightly. In a mixing bowl, combine cream cheese, chocolate syrup and sugar until blended. Fold in whipped topping. Spread over cake. Sprinkle with crushed Heath bars. Cover and refrigerate for at least 1 hour. Garnish with additional Heath bars if desired. **Yield:** 16-20 servings.

Pink Lemonade Dessert

This refreshing treat is light and cool and goes very well after a big meal. Plus, you can make it ahead. —Nancy McDonald, Burns, Wyoming

 2 cups crushed butter-flavored crackers
   (about 50)
 1/4 cup confectioners' sugar
 1/2 cup butter, melted
 1 can (14 ounces) sweetened condensed
   milk
 3/4 cup pink lemonade concentrate
 1 carton (12 ounces) frozen whipped
   topping, thawed
 2 to 3 teaspoons red food coloring,
   optional

In a bowl, combine cracker crumbs and sugar. Stir in butter. Press into a greased 13-in. x 9-in. x 2-in. dish; set aside.

In a blender or food processor, combine milk and lemonade concentrate; cover and process until well blended. Fold in the whipped topping and food coloring if desired. Spread evenly over crust. Cover and refrigerate for 2 hours or until firm. **Yield:** 12 servings.

Ice Cream
& Toppings

Lemon Ice, p. 105

Mint Chip Ice Cream

(Pictured below)

We have a milk cow, so homemade ice cream has become a regular treat for our family. This version is very creamy with a mild mint flavor that goes well with the mini chocolate chips. It was an instant hit with my husband and our two little girls.
—Farrah McGuire, Springdale, Washington

3 eggs, lightly beaten
1-3/4 cups milk
3/4 cup sugar
Pinch salt
1-3/4 cups heavy whipping cream
1 teaspoon vanilla extract
1/4 teaspoon peppermint extract
4 drops green food coloring, optional
1/2 cup miniature semisweet chocolate chips

In a saucepan, combine the eggs, milk, sugar and salt. Cook and stir over medium heat until mixture reaches 160° and coats a metal spoon. Cool to room temperature. Stir in cream, vanilla, peppermint extract and food coloring if desired. Refrigerate for 2 hours.

Stir in the chocolate chips. Fill ice cream freezer cylinder two-thirds full; freeze according to the manufacturer's directions. Refrigerate remaining mixture until ready to freeze. **Yield:** 1-1/2 quarts.

Hot Fudge Sauce

The big chocolate flavor of this heavenly sauce over ice cream and a brownie is sure to satisfy the craving of any sweet tooth. *—Priscilla Weaver*
Hagerstown, Maryland

1 can (14 ounces) sweetened condensed milk
4 squares (1 ounce *each*) semisweet chocolate
2 tablespoons butter
1 teaspoon vanilla extract

In a heavy saucepan, combine the milk, chocolate and butter. Cook and stir over medium-low heat until chocolate is melted. Remove from the heat; stir in vanilla. **Yield:** about 1-1/2 cups.

Caramel Banana Sundaes

When I don't have time to bake, I often rely on this quick dessert. *—Jeanne Mays*
North Richland Hills, Texas

3 tablespoons brown sugar
2 tablespoons butter
2 tablespoons heavy whipping cream
1/2 teaspoon rum extract
1/2 teaspoon vanilla extract
1/4 teaspoon ground cinnamon
2 medium firm bananas, cut into 1/2-inch slices
Vanilla ice cream

In a skillet, combine brown sugar, butter, cream, extracts and cinnamon. Bring to a boil over medium heat, stirring constantly. Cook for 2 minutes. Remove from the heat; add bananas and stir until coated. Return to heat; cook 2 minutes longer, stirring occasionally. Serve warm over ice cream. **Yield:** 4 servings.

German Chocolate Ice Cream

I found this recipe years ago and have been taking it to ice cream socials ever since. But you won't want to wait for a get-together to enjoy it. The cool combination of chocolate, coconut and pecans is delicious anytime. *—Peggy Key*
Grant, Alabama

1-1/2 cups sugar
1/4 cup all-purpose flour

1/4 teaspoon ground cinnamon
1/4 teaspoon salt
   4 cups milk
   3 eggs, beaten
   1 quart half-and-half cream
   2 packages (4 ounces *each*) German
      sweet chocolate, melted
   1 cup flaked coconut
   1 cup chopped pecans

In a large heavy saucepan, combine the sugar, flour, cinnamon and salt. Gradually add milk and eggs; stir until smooth. Cook and stir over medium-low heat until mixture is thick enough to coat a metal spoon and reaches 160°, about 15 minutes. Stir in the remaining ingredients. Refrigerate for several hours or overnight.

Fill ice cream freezer cylinder two-thirds full; freeze according to manufacturer's instructions. Refrigerate remaining mixture until ready to freeze. Remove ice cream from the freezer 10 minutes before serving. **Yield:** 1 gallon.

Lemon Ice

(Pictured on page 103)

Pucker up for this sweet-tart treat. The delicious lemon dessert is a perfectly refreshing way to end a summer meal…or any meal, for that matter.
— Concetta Maranto Skenfield
Bakersfield, California

   2 cups sugar
   1 cup water
   2 cups lemon juice
   1 tablespoon grated lemon peel

In a saucepan over low heat, cook and stir sugar and water until sugar is dissolved. Remove from the heat and stir in the lemon juice. Pour into a freezer container.

Freeze for 4 hours, stirring every 30 minutes, or until mixture becomes slushy. Sprinkle servings with lemon peel. **Yield:** 6 servings.

Ice Cream Social

For a fun dessert sure to impress guests, roll individually frozen balls of ice cream in fun toppings like chopped nuts, toasted coconut or chopped candy bars. Then freeze the balls until firm and arrange in a pretty serving bowl. Guests can choose whichever combination appeals to them.

Refreshing Lime Sherbet

(Pictured above)

One spoonful of this cool, fresh-tasting and delicious treat and you'll never eat store-bought lime sherbet again! It's terrific following a heavy meal, on a hot summer day or anytime your taste buds are bored.
— Lorraine Searing
Colorado Springs, Colorado

4-1/4 cups sugar
1-1/2 cups lime juice
   3 tablespoons lemon juice
   2 tablespoons grated lime peel
7-1/2 cups milk
   1/2 cup buttermilk
   1 drop green food coloring, optional

In a bowl, combine sugar, lime juice, lemon juice and lime peel until well blended. Gradually stir in milk, buttermilk and food coloring if desired; mix well. Pour into the cylinder of an ice cream freezer and freeze according to manufacturer's directions. Remove from the freezer 10 minutes before serving. **Yield:** about 2-1/2 quarts.

Editor's Note: Recipe may need to be frozen in two batches.

1 cup sugar
2/3 cup water
2 cups fresh *or* frozen cranberries
2/3 cup orange juice
1/2 teaspoon grated orange peel
1/2 teaspoon vanilla extract
Vanilla ice cream
Additional orange peel, optional

In a saucepan over medium heat, bring sugar and water to a boil; cook for 5 minutes. Add cranberries, orange juice and peel. Return to a boil. Reduce heat; simmer for 8-10 minutes or until berries pop. Remove from the heat; stir in vanilla. Serve warm or chilled over ice cream. Garnish with orange peel if desired. **Yield:** 2 cups.

Gingered Pear Sorbet

During the hot summer here we enjoy this refreshing sorbet. Sometimes I dress up servings with berries, mint leaves or crystallized ginger.
—Donna Cline, Pensacola, Florida

1 can (29 ounces) pear halves
1/4 cup sugar
2 tablespoons lemon juice
1/8 teaspoon ground ginger
Yellow food coloring, optional

Drain pears, reserving 1 cup syrup (discard remaining syrup or save for another use); set pears aside. In a saucepan, bring sugar and reserved syrup to a boil. Remove from the heat; cool.

In a blender, process the pears, lemon juice and ginger until smooth. Add cooled syrup and food coloring if desired; cover and process until pureed. Pour into an 11-in. x 7-in. x 2-in. dish. Cover and freeze for 1-1/2 to 2 hours or until partially frozen.

Return mixture to blender; cover and process until smooth. Place in a freezer container; cover and freeze for at least 3 hours. Remove from the freezer 20 minutes before serving. **Yield:** 3 cups.

Chocolate Praline Ice Cream Topping

(Pictured above)

Friends tell me they look forward to ice cream socials just to have this topping. —*Angie Zalewski Dripping Springs, Texas*

1 cup heavy whipping cream
2/3 cup packed brown sugar
2/3 cup butter
1 cup (6 ounces) semisweet chocolate chips
1 cup chopped pecans
Ice cream

In a saucepan over medium heat, bring cream, brown sugar and butter to a boil, stirring constantly. Reduce heat; simmer for 2 minutes, stirring occasionally. Remove from the heat; stir in the chocolate chips until melted and smooth. Stir in pecans. Serve warm over ice cream. Store in the refrigerator. **Yield:** 3 cups.

Cranberry Orange Sundaes

I always keep a supply of cranberries in the freezer to cook up this refreshing sauce year-round.
—Rita Goshaw, South Milwaukee, Wisconsin

Peanut Butter Ice Cream Topping

Whenever there's an ice cream social at church, this scrumptious topping is requested. It's easy to make. —*Karen Buhr, Gasport, New York*

1 cup packed brown sugar
1/2 cup light corn syrup
3 tablespoons butter
Pinch salt

1 cup creamy peanut butter
1/2 cup evaporated milk
Vanilla ice cream
Peanuts, optional

Combine brown sugar, corn syrup, butter and salt in a 1-1/2-qt. microwave-safe baking dish. Cover and microwave on high for 4 minutes or until mixture boils, stirring twice. Add peanut butter; stir until smooth. Stir in evaporated milk. Serve warm over ice cream. Sprinkle with peanuts if desired. Cover and store in the refrigerator. **Yield:** 2-3/4 cups.

Editor's Note: This recipe was tested using a 700-watt microwave.

Banana Ice Cream

I remember this ice cream from summer holidays at my grandparents' lake cottage.
—Tammy Mikesell, Columbia City, Indiana

3 eggs, beaten
3 cups sugar
6 cups cold milk, *divided*
1 package (3.4 ounces) instant vanilla pudding mix
1 cup orange juice
1 cup lemon juice
1 cup mashed ripe bananas (2 to 3 medium)
4 cups half-and-half cream

In a saucepan, combine the eggs, sugar and 4 cups milk. Cook and stir over medium heat until the mixture reaches 160° and is thick enough to coat a metal spoon. Cool.

Meanwhile, in a mixing bowl, combine pudding mix and remaining milk. Beat on low speed for 2 minutes. Stir juices, bananas, cream and pudding into cooled egg mixture. Freeze in batches in an ice cream freezer according to manufacturer's instructions. Refrigerate extra mixture until it can be frozen. **Yield:** about 3-1/2 quarts.

Pineapple Cherry Ice Cream

I use an ice cream freezer to make this colorful crowd-pleaser, which is sure to be a success wherever it's served. —Johanna Gimmeson
Powell, Wyoming

2-1/2 cups sugar
1 package (6 ounces) cherry gelatin
2 cups boiling water

4 cups milk
4 cups heavy whipping cream
1 can (20 ounces) crushed pineapple, drained
1/3 cup lemon juice

In a bowl, dissolve sugar and gelatin in boiling water. Refrigerate for 1 hour or until cool. Stir in the milk, cream, pineapple and lemon juice; mix well. Fill cylinder of ice cream freezer two-thirds full; freeze according to manufacturer's directions. Refrigerate remaining mixture until ready to freeze. **Yield:** 3 quarts.

Srawberry Ice

(Pictured below)

When we pick strawberries at a local farm, this is what many of the berries are used for.
—Kim Hammond, Watsonville, California

5 cups fresh *or* frozen unsweetened strawberries
2/3 cup sugar
2/3 cup water
1/4 cup lemon juice

Place the strawberries in a blender or food processor; cover and process until smooth. In a saucepan, heat sugar and water until sugar is dissolved; pour into blender. Add lemon juice; cover and process until combined.

Pour into a shallow freezer container; cover and freeze for 4-6 hours or until almost frozen. Just before serving, whip mixture in a blender or food processor. **Yield:** 6 servings.

Grape Sherbet

My husband, two daughters and I enjoyed this refreshing treat at our friends' house. They graciously shared the recipe after we all raved about it.
—Sherry Rominger, Rogers, Arkansas

1-3/4 cups grape juice
3 tablespoons lemon juice
1/2 cup sugar
1-3/4 cups half-and-half cream

In a large bowl, combine all ingredients. Pour into the cylinder of a 1-qt. ice cream freezer; freeze according to manufacturer's directions. Allow to ripen in ice cream freezer or in refrigerator freezer for 2-4 hours before serving. **Yield:** 1 quart.

Coconut Ice Cream

(Pictured below)

This is a refreshing dessert that can cap off a warm summer evening. It has a nice coconut flavor without being too strong. —Tamra Kriedeman
Enderlin, North Dakota

1-3/4 cups sugar
1/2 teaspoon salt
4 cups milk

1-1/2 cups flaked coconut, *divided*
4 cups heavy whipping cream
1 tablespoon vanilla extract
Toasted flaked coconut, optional

In a saucepan, combine the sugar, salt and milk; cook and stir over medium heat just until mixture begins to boil. Stir in 1/2 cup coconut. Remove from the heat; let stand for 30 minutes. Strain, discarding coconut.

Place milk mixture in a large bowl; add cream, vanilla and remaining coconut. Freeze in an ice cream freezer according to manufacturer's directions. Transfer to a 2-qt. freezer container. Cover and freeze for at least 4 hours before serving. Garnish with toasted coconut if desired. **Yield:** 2 quarts.

Creamy Citrus Sherbet

This recipe was handwritten in a booklet that came with my family's first refrigerator in the early 1940s. I was very young at the time, but I can still remember the iceman delivering huge blocks of ice. Since finding the booklet among my mother's things, I make this refreshing dessert often.
—Maribelle Culver
Grand Rapids, Michigan

2 cups sugar
1-1/2 cups orange juice
5 tablespoons lemon juice
4 cups milk

In a large bowl, combine sugar and juices. Gradually add milk. Pour into a 2-qt. freezer container. Freeze for 1 hour, then stir every 30 minutes until slushy. Freeze overnight. **Yield:** about 2 quarts.

Noel Ice Cream Cups

Each Christmas, our family enjoys a dessert that's much more fun than the typical pies and cakes. With refreshing ice cream chock-full of holiday ingredients like nuts, cherries and candies, these treats are a delightful end to a perfect meal.
—Dorothy Anderson, Ottawa, Kansas

1 quart vanilla ice cream, softened
1/4 cup chopped pecans, toasted
2 tablespoons *each* chopped red and
green maraschino cherries
1 teaspoon vanilla extract
1/2 teaspoon almond extract
1/2 cup M&M's
Additional M&M's, chopped

In a medium bowl, combine the ice cream, pecans, cherries and extracts; mix well. Fold in M&M's. Spoon into paper-lined muffin cups and freeze for at least 30 minutes. Sprinkle with chopped M&M's. **Yield:** 8-10 servings.

German Chocolate Sundaes

This terrific topping is a real treat over chocolate ice cream. It's fun and fancy at the same time and much cooler to make on hot days than a German chocolate cake. —DeEtta Rasmussen
Fort Madison, Iowa

  1/2 cup sugar
  1/2 cup evaporated milk
  1/4 cup butter
    2 egg yolks, beaten
  2/3 cup flaked coconut
  1/2 cup chopped pecans
    1 teaspoon vanilla extract
Chocolate ice cream
Chocolate syrup, toasted coconut and
  additional chopped pecans, optional

In a heavy saucepan, combine the sugar, milk, butter and egg yolks. Bring to a boil over medium heat, stirring constantly; cook and stir for 2 minutes or until thickened.

Remove from the heat. Stir in the coconut, pecans and vanilla. Stir until sauce is cooled slightly. Serve over ice cream. Top with chocolate syrup, coconut and pecans if desired. **Yield:** 1-1/4 cups.

Cranberry Ice

I've enjoyed this with turkey at Christmas since I was a child. But it also makes a delicious dessert.
—Eleanor Dunbar, Peoria, Illinois

  4 cups fresh *or* frozen cranberries
  4 cups cold water, *divided*
  1 package (3 ounces) lemon-flavored
    gelatin
  2 cups boiling water
  3 cups sugar
  1/2 cup lemon juice
  1/2 cup orange juice

In a saucepan, bring cranberries and 2 cups cold water to a boil. Reduce heat; simmer for 5 minutes. Press through a strainer to remove skins; set juice aside and discard skins. In a bowl, stir gelatin, boiling water and sugar until dissolved. Add cranberry juice, lemon and orange juices and remain-

ing cold water. Pour into a 13-in. x 9-in. x 2-in. pan. Cover and freeze until ice begins to form around the edges of the pan, about 1-1/2 hours; stir. Freeze until mushy, about 30 minutes. Spoon into a freezer container; cover and freeze. **Yield:** 20 servings.

Butter Pecan Sauce

(Pictured above)

It's hard to beat the homemade goodness of this buttery smooth pecan sauce over ice cream.
—Kim Gilliland, Simi Valley, California

  1/2 cup plus 2 tablespoons packed brown
    sugar
    2 tablespoons sugar
    4 teaspoons cornstarch
  3/4 cup heavy whipping cream
    1 tablespoon butter
  1/2 cup chopped pecans, toasted
Vanilla ice cream *or* flavor of your choice

In a heavy saucepan, combine the sugars and cornstarch. Gradually stir in cream until smooth. Bring to a boil over medium heat, stirring constantly; cook and stir for 2-3 minutes or until slightly thickened. Remove from the heat; stir in butter until melted. Add the pecans. Serve warm over ice cream. **Yield:** 1-1/2 cups.

Lemon Ice Cream

Both of my grown daughters look for this ice cream when they visit. I love this recipe because it's delicious and not at all tricky to make.
—Nancy Schantz, San Angelo, Texas

> 1 package (3 ounces) cream cheese, softened
> 3 cups sugar
> 1 package (3 ounces) lemon gelatin
> 2 cups half-and-half cream
> 2/3 cup lemon juice
> 1 teaspoon vanilla extract
> 1/2 teaspoon lemon extract
> 1 cup heavy whipping cream, whipped
> 8 to 10 cups milk
> Yellow food coloring, optional

In a mixing bowl, combine the cream cheese, sugar and gelatin; mix well. Add half-and-half, lemon juice and extracts; beat until smooth. Fold in the whipped cream. Stir in enough milk to measure 1 gallon. Add food coloring if desired.

Freeze in batches according to manufacturer's directions. Refrigerate extra mixture until it can be frozen. Allow to ripen in ice cream freezer or firm up in refrigerator freezer for 2-4 hours before serving. Remove from freezer 10 minutes before serving. **Yield:** 1 gallon.

Coffee Ice Cream

(Pictured above)

I combined two recipes—one for vanilla ice cream and the other for a special coffee sauce—to create this one. I serve it plain, just scooped into a dessert dish, so the mild, creamy coffee flavor can be enjoyed to the fullest. —Theresa Hansen
Pensacola, Florida

> 1/4 cup sugar
> 1 tablespoon cornstarch
> 1 tablespoon instant coffee granules
> 2 tablespoons butter, melted
> 1 cup milk
> 1 teaspoon vanilla extract
> 1 can (14 ounces) sweetened condensed milk
> 2 cups heavy whipping cream

In a saucepan, stir sugar, cornstarch, coffee and butter until blended. Stir in milk. Bring to a boil over medium heat; cook and stir for 2 minutes or until thickened. Remove from the heat; stir in vanilla. Cool completely.

Stir in condensed milk. In a mixing bowl, beat cream until stiff peaks form; fold into milk mixture. Pour into a 9-in. square pan. Cover and freeze for 6 hours or until firm. **Yield:** 1-1/2 quarts.

Vanilla Custard Ice Cream

My husband and I used to run a dairy farm, so many of my recipes call for dairy products. This is the most wonderful custard I've ever had...and my family and guests have loved it for years.
—Margaret Gage, Roseboom, New York

> 2 eggs, beaten
> 2 cups milk
> 3/4 cup sugar
> 1/8 teaspoon salt
> 2 cups heavy whipping cream
> 2 tablespoons vanilla extract
> Colored sprinkles, optional

In a large saucepan, combine the eggs, milk, sugar and salt. Cook and stir over medium-low heat until the mixture reaches 160° and is thick enough to coat a metal spoon. Cool. Stir in the whipping cream and vanilla.

Fill cylinder of ice cream freezer two-thirds full; freeze according to manufacturer's directions. Refrigerate remaining mixture until ready to freeze. Allow to ripen in ice cream freezer or firm up in refrigerator freezer for 2-4 hours before serving. Garnish with colored sprinkles if desired. **Yield:** 1-1/2 quarts.

Georgia Peach Ice Cream

My state is well known for growing good peaches. This delicious recipe has been a family favorite for almost 50 years. —Marguerite Ethridge
Americus, Georgia

```
    1 quart milk
    4 eggs
2-1/4 cups sugar, divided
  1/2 teaspoon salt
    2 cans (14 ounces each) sweetened
      condensed milk
1-3/4 pounds fresh peaches, peeled and
      sliced
Fresh mint, optional
```

In a heavy saucepan, bring milk to a boil. Meanwhile, beat eggs. Add 1 cup sugar and salt; mix well. Gradually add a small amount of hot milk to egg mixture; return all to the pan. Cook over medium-low heat, stirring constantly, until mixture is thick enough to coat a metal spoon and reaches at least 160°, about 6-8 minutes.

Remove from the heat. Set pan in ice and stir the mixture for 5-10 minutes. Gradually stir in condensed milk; mix well. Cover and refrigerate overnight. When ready to freeze, mash peaches with remaining sugar in a small bowl; let stand for 30 minutes. Combine milk mixture and peaches in an ice cream freezer. Freeze according to manufacturer's directions. Garnish with mint if desired. **Yield:** 3-3/4 quarts.

Three-Fruit Sundae Sauce

We brought back some rhubarb from a trip to Wisconsin. I dreamed up this bright-red sauce that blends rhubarb with strawberries and oranges.
—Sharron Trefren, Grand Bay, Alabama

```
2 cups sugar
2 tablespoons cornstarch
6 cups chopped fresh or frozen rhubarb
2 cups fresh or frozen unsweetened
    sliced strawberries
2 medium navel oranges, peeled and
    sectioned
1 teaspoon grated lemon peel
3 cups water
1 cinnamon stick (3 inches)
Vanilla ice cream
```

In a large saucepan, combine the sugar, cornstarch, rhubarb, strawberries, oranges and lemon peel until blended. Stir in the water and cinnamon stick. Bring to a boil; cook and stir for 2 minutes.

Reduce heat; simmer, uncovered, for 50-60 minutes or until thickened. Discard cinnamon stick.

Cool. Refrigerate until chilled. Serve over the ice cream. **Yield:** 7 cups.

Editor's Note: If using frozen rhubarb, measure rhubarb while still frozen, then thaw completely. Drain in a colander, but do not press liquid out.

Mocha Ice Cream

(Pictured below)

Here's a recipe for chocolate ice cream that I've enjoyed for over 40 years. Coffee really enhances the flavor. —Dick McCarty
Lake Havasu City, Arizona

```
2-1/4 cups sugar
  3/4 cup baking cocoa
  1/3 cup all-purpose flour
    1 tablespoon instant coffee granules
Dash salt
    3 cups milk
    4 eggs, beaten
    4 cups half-and-half cream
    2 cups heavy whipping cream
    3 tablespoons vanilla extract
```

In a large heavy saucepan, combine the sugar, cocoa, flour, coffee and salt. Gradually add milk and eggs; stir until smooth. Cook and stir over medium-low heat until mixture is thick enough to coat a metal spoon and reaches 160°, about 15 minutes.

Refrigerate until chilled. Stir in the remaining ingredients. Fill ice cream freezer cylinder two-thirds full; freeze according to manufacturer's instructions. Refrigerate remaining mixture until ready to freeze. Remove from the freezer 10 minutes before serving. **Yield:** about 2-1/2 quarts.

Chocolate Ice Cream Sandwiches

These cute chewy cookies made with two kinds of chocolate form a perfect sandwich for vanilla ice cream...or any flavor ice cream you prefer.
—Michelle Wolford, San Antonio, Texas

1/3 cup butter, softened
1/3 cup sugar
1/3 cup packed brown sugar
1 egg
1/2 teaspoon vanilla extract
3/4 cup plus 2 tablespoons all-purpose flour
1/4 cup baking cocoa
1/2 teaspoon baking powder
1/4 teaspoon baking soda
1/4 teaspoon salt
1/2 cup semisweet chocolate chips
1 pint vanilla ice cream

In a mixing bowl, cream butter and sugars. Beat in the egg and vanilla. Combine the flour, cocoa, baking powder, baking soda and salt; add to creamed mixture and mix well.

Drop by rounded tablespoonfuls 2 in. apart onto greased baking sheets, forming 16 cookies. Flatten slightly with a glass. Sprinkle with chocolate chips. Bake at 375° for 8-10 minutes or until set. Remove to wire racks to cool.

To assemble sandwiches, place 1/4 cup ice cream on the bottom of half the cookies. Top with remaining cookies. Wrap each in plastic wrap. Freeze overnight. **Yield:** 8 ice cream sandwiches.

Apple Streusel Ice Cream

If you're a fan of apple pie, you'll be sweet on this delicious ice cream. The creamy concoction is flavored with sauteed apple, cinnamon, caramel topping and a homemade streusel mixture.
—Karen Delgado, Shawnee, Kansas

1/3 cup packed brown sugar
1/4 cup all-purpose flour
1/2 teaspoon ground cinnamon
3 tablespoons plus 4-1/2 teaspoons cold butter, *divided*
1/2 cup chopped pecans
1 cup chopped peeled Golden Delicious apple
2 teaspoons sugar
1/4 teaspoon ground cinnamon
ICE CREAM:
1-1/4 cups milk
3/4 cup sugar
1-3/4 cups heavy whipping cream
1-1/2 teaspoons vanilla extract
1 jar (12 ounces) caramel ice cream topping

For streusel, combine the brown sugar, flour and cinnamon in a bowl; cut in 3 tablespoons butter until mixture resembles coarse crumbs. Stir in pecans. Press into a 9-in. pie plate. Bake at 350° for 10-12 minutes or until the edges are browned. Cool slightly; break into small pieces. Cool completely.

In a skillet, melt remaining butter. Stir in the apple, sugar and cinnamon. Cook for 8-10 minutes or until apple is tender; cool.

In a large saucepan, heat the milk to 175°; stir in sugar until dissolved. Cool. In a large bowl, combine the milk mixture, cream and vanilla. Refrigerate for several hours or overnight.

Fill cylinder of ice cream freezer two-thirds full; freeze according to the manufacturer's directions. Refrigerate remaining mixture until ready to freeze. Add apple mixture to each batch of ice cream; freeze 5 minutes longer.

Spoon a third of the ice cream into a freezer container. Top with a third of the streusel mixture. Drizzle with a third of the caramel topping. Repeat layers once. Top with remaining ice cream. With a spatula, cut through ice cream in several places to gently swirl layers. Cover; freeze overnight. Garnish with the remaining streusel and caramel topping. **Yield:** 1-1/2 quarts.

Brownie Sundaes

With prepared brownies, I can fix this sweet treat in a flash. For extra flair, I roll the ice cream in pecans before placing them on top of the brownies.
—Ruth Lee, Troy, Ontario

3/4 cup semisweet chocolate chips
1/2 cup evaporated milk
2 tablespoons brown sugar
2 teaspoons butter
1/2 teaspoon vanilla extract
6 prepared brownies (3 inches square)
6 scoops vanilla *or* **chocolate fudge ice cream**
1/2 cup chopped pecans

In a saucepan, combine the chocolate chips, milk and brown sugar. Cook and stir over medium heat for 5 minutes or until chocolate is melted and sugar is dissolved. Remove from the heat; stir in butter and vanilla.

Spoon about 2 tablespoons warm chocolate sauce onto each dessert plate. Top with a brownie and a scoop of ice cream. Drizzle with additional chocolate sauce if desired. Sprinkle with pecans. **Yield:** 6 servings.

Rocky Road Freeze

Summertime offers all sorts of delights—and none of them is more eagerly anticipated than ice cream! That dairy-good dessert was the refreshingly cool focus of our Ice Cream Social contest.

There was lots of lip smacking as our taste panel dug into homemade ice creams, sherbets and freezes, poured on delectable sauces and munched tasty toppings. After the last spoon had been licked clean came the difficult part—selecting the Grand Prize Winner.

That honor went to Sheila Berry of Carrying Place, Ontario, for her chocolaty Rocky Road Freeze. "The first time I served it at a dinner party, it was a big hit," says Sheila. "Everyone raved about the rich taste. Still, they hesitated before asking for my recipe. They figured homemade ice cream would be just too complicated. So they were pleasantly surprised to learn how easy it is. In fact, my Rocky Road Freeze is ideal for anyone making ice cream for the first time."

—Sheila Berry, Carrying Place, Ontario

- **1 can (14 ounces) sweetened condensed milk**
- **1/2 cup chocolate syrup**
- **2 cups heavy whipping cream**
- **1 cup miniature marshmallows**
- **1/2 cup miniature chocolate chips**
- **1/2 cup chopped salted peanuts**

In a small bowl, combine the milk and chocolate syrup; set aside. In a mixing bowl, beat cream until stiff peaks form. Fold in chocolate mixture, marshmallows, chocolate chips and peanuts.

Transfer to a freezer-proof container; cover and freeze for 5 hours or until firm. Remove from freezer 10 minutes before serving. **Yield:** about 1-1/2 quarts.

Sunshine Sherbet

Together, my mother and I "invented" this recipe. Warm, humid evenings in Georgia, where I grew up, were all the inspiration we needed! It became a favorite part of gatherings with family and friends. After I got married, my boys and their pals would all be there when the sherbet left the freezer. Today my grandkids love to dig into bowls of it as well.

—Barbara Looney, Fort Knox, Kentucky

- **2 cups sugar**
- **1-1/2 cups water**
- **2 cups milk**
- **2 cups heavy whipping cream**
- **1-1/2 cups orange juice**
- **1 can (12 ounces) evaporated milk**
- **1/3 cup lemon juice**
- **2 teaspoons grated orange peel**
- **8 drops red food coloring, optional**
- **1/2 teaspoon yellow food coloring, optional**

In a saucepan over medium heat, bring sugar and water to a boil; boil for 5 minutes. Cool completely. Add remaining ingredients; mix well.

Pour into the cylinder of an ice cream freezer and freeze according to the manufacturer's directions. Remove from the freezer 10 minutes before serving. **Yield:** about 2 quarts.

Homemade Ice Cream Sandwiches

My mom sent me this recipe. We love it, and so does company I serve it to. I inherited my love of cooking from my mother. She's a former home economics teacher. When we were growing up, each of us kids had one night a week when we prepared supper for the rest of the family.
—Kea Fisher, Bridger, Montana

    1 **package (18-1/4 ounces) chocolate cake mix**
1/4 **cup shortening**
1/4 **cup butter, softened**
    1 **egg**
    1 **tablespoon water**
    1 **teaspoon vanilla extract**
1/2 **gallon ice cream**

In a mixing bowl, combine cake mix, shortening, butter, egg, water and vanilla; beat until well blended. Divide into four equal parts. Between waxed paper, roll one part into a 10-in. x 6-in. rectangle. Remove one piece of waxed paper and flip dough onto an ungreased baking sheet. Score the dough into eight pieces, each 3 in. x 2-1/2 in. Repeat with remaining dough. Bake at 350° for 8-10 minutes or until puffed.

Immediately cut along the scored lines and prick holes in each piece with a fork; cool on baking sheets. Cut ice cream into 16 slices, each 3 in. x 2-1/2 in. x 1 in. Place ice cream between two chocolate cookies; wrap in plastic wrap. Freeze on a baking sheet overnight. Store in an airtight container. **Yield:** 16 servings.

Editor's Note: Purchase a rectangular-shaped package of ice cream in the flavor of your choice for the easiest cutting.

Peach Melba Ice Cream Pie

On a hot night, this pie makes a very refreshing dessert. Like most wonderful recipes, it came from a friend. As the third-oldest among nine children, I've been cooking for a crowd as long as I can remember! This pie has long been a favorite.
—Judy Vaske, Bancroft, Iowa

1-1/2 **cups flaked coconut**
  1/3 **cup chopped pecans**
    3 **tablespoons butter, melted**
    1 **quart frozen peach yogurt, softened**
    1 **pint vanilla ice cream, softened**
    1 **tablespoon cornstarch**
    1 **tablespoon sugar**
    1 **package (10 ounces) frozen raspberries in syrup, thawed**
    1 **cup sliced fresh or frozen peaches, thawed**

Combine coconut, pecans and butter; press onto the bottom and up the sides of an ungreased 9-in. pie plate. Bake at 350° for 12 minutes or until crust begins to brown around edges. Cool completely.

Spoon frozen yogurt into crust; smooth the top. Spread ice cream over yogurt. Cover and freeze for 2 hours or until firm.

In a small saucepan, combine cornstarch and sugar; drain raspberry juice into pan. Bring to a boil; cook and stir for 2 minutes. Remove from the heat; add raspberries. Cover and chill.

Remove the pie from the freezer 10 minutes before serving. Arrange the peaches on top of the pie; drizzle with a little of the sauce. Pass the remaining sauce around with slices of the pie. **Yield:** 6-8 servings.

Brownie Ice Cream Cones

Often, I'll find a recipe that sounds interesting, copy it down and put my own twist on it. That's just what I did with these. I make them for our children when they have friends over. They love the combination of a brownie and ice cream in a cone.
—Marlene Rhodes, Panama City, Florida

    1 package (4 ounces) German sweet
      chocolate
  1/4 cup butter
  3/4 cup sugar
    2 eggs
  1/2 cup all-purpose flour
  1/2 cup chopped walnuts, optional
    1 teaspoon vanilla extract
   24 cake ice cream cones (about 3 inches
      tall)
   24 scoops ice cream
Colored or chocolate sprinkles

In a saucepan over low heat, melt the chocolate and butter, stirring frequently. Cool slightly; pour into a bowl. Add sugar and eggs; mix well. Stir in flour, walnuts if desired and vanilla.

Place the ice cream cones in muffin cups; fill half full with batter. Bake at 350° for 20-22 minutes or until brownies are set on top and a toothpick inserted near the center comes out with moist crumbs (do not overbake). Cool completely.

Just before serving, top each with a scoop of ice cream and garnish with sprinkles. **Yield:** 2 dozen.

prize winning tips

* * * * *

*A popular dessert at our house is one part angel food cake chunks combined with two parts softened ice cream. Serve with the topping of your choice.
—Mary McCreery, Boynton Beach, Florida

*To soften ice cream topping that has been refrigerated, I place the can or jar in hot water until it's pourable. You can also put the topping in a microwave-safe dish and heat it in the microwave for just a few seconds.
—Nancy Newton, Greendale, Wisconsin

*If you'd like to prevent a sticky coating, put plastic wrap directly on top of ice cream in the container when you freeze it.
—Beverly Matheson, Taylorsville, Utah

Berry Good Ice Cream Sauce

I started cooking in earnest as a bride over 40 years ago. I'm thankful to say I improved in time—though I made something once even the dog refused to eat! Now, my three children are grown and I'm a grandmother. My grandkids love this sauce on top of vanilla ice cream.

—Joy Beck, Cincinnati, Ohio

1-3/4 cups sliced fresh or frozen rhubarb
2/3 cup pureed fresh or frozen strawberries
1/4 cup sugar
1/4 cup orange juice
2 cups sliced fresh or frozen strawberries
Vanilla ice cream

In a saucepan, combine the first four ingredients. Cook over medium heat until rhubarb is tender, about 5 minutes. Stir in the sliced strawberries. Store in the refrigerator. Serve over ice cream. **Yield:** 3-1/2 cups.

Caramel Fried Ice Cream

At times, I substitute strawberry or Neapolitan for the vanilla ice cream. Our children used to love eating out at Mexican restaurants just so they could order fried ice cream for dessert. When I came upon this recipe, I copied it down quickly!

—Darlene Markel, Sublimity, Oregon

1 quart vanilla ice cream
1/4 cup heavy whipping cream
2 teaspoons vanilla extract
2 cups flaked coconut, finely chopped
2 cups finely crushed cornflakes
1/2 teaspoon ground cinnamon
CARAMEL SAUCE:
1 cup sugar
1/2 cup butter
1/2 cup evaporated milk
Oil for deep-fat frying

Using a 1/2-cup ice cream scoop, place eight scoops of ice cream on a baking sheet. Cover and freeze for 2 hours or until firm. In a bowl, combine cream and vanilla. In another bowl, combine coconut, cornflakes and cinnamon. Remove ice cream from freezer; wearing plastic gloves, shape the ice cream into balls. Dip balls into cream mixture, then roll in coconut mixture, making sure to coat entire surface. Place coated balls on a baking sheet. Cover and freeze 3 hours or until firm.

For caramel sauce, heat sugar in a heavy saucepan over medium heat until partially melted and golden, stirring occasionally. Add butter. Gradually add milk, stirring constantly. Cook and stir for 8 minutes or until sauce is thick and golden; keep warm.

Heat oil in an electric skillet or deep-fat fryer to 375°. Fry ice cream balls until golden, about 30 seconds. Drain on paper towels. Serve immediately with caramel sauce. **Yield:** 8 servings.

Fruit
Desserts

Strawberry Peach Melba, p. 120

Peach Cake Dessert

(Pictured below)

This dessert is very good served with whipped cream or ice cream. —Virginia Slater
West Sunbury, Pennsylvania

> 1 cup sugar
> 1 tablespoon all-purpose flour
> 1 to 2 teaspoons ground cinnamon
> 5 medium fresh peaches, peeled and sliced

CAKE:
> 1/4 cup butter, softened
> 1/2 cup sugar
> 1 egg
> 1 cup all-purpose flour
> 2 teaspoons baking powder
> 1/4 teaspoon salt
> 1/4 cup milk

In a bowl, combine sugar, flour and cinnamon. Add peaches and toss to coat. Transfer to a greased 8-in. square baking pan.

In a mixing bowl, cream butter and sugar. Beat in egg. Combine flour, baking powder and salt; add to the creamed mixture alternately with milk. Drop by spoonfuls onto peaches; spread evenly. Bake at 350° for 40-45 minutes or until a toothpick inserted near the center comes out clean. Serve warm. **Yield:** 6 servings.

Spiced Oranges

This refreshing fruit cup makes a delightfully different dessert. The orange sections, spiced with cloves and cinnamon, can be prepared ahead and kept in the fridge until serving. —Sue Ross
Casa Grande, Arizona

> 1/4 cup red wine *or* grape juice
> 3 tablespoons water
> 2 tablespoons honey
> 1 lemon slice
> 1 small cinnamon stick (1 inch)
> 1 whole clove
> 2 medium oranges, peeled and sectioned

Fresh mint, optional

In a saucepan, combine the first six ingredients. Cook over medium heat until slightly thickened, about 15 minutes. Add oranges; simmer for 1 minute. Pour into a bowl; refrigerate. Discard lemon, cinnamon and clove before serving. Garnish with mint if desired. **Yield:** 2 servings.

Blackberry Custard Torte

Blackberries are my husband's favorite fruit, so I make this outstanding dessert especially for him. It's well worth the effort. —Ann Fox, Austin, Texas

> 1 cup all-purpose flour
> 1/2 cup sugar
> 1-1/2 teaspoons baking powder
> 1/2 cup cold butter
> 1 egg

FILLING:
> 3 egg yolks
> 2 cups (16 ounces) sour cream
> 1/2 cup sugar
> 1/4 teaspoon vanilla extract
> 4 cups fresh *or* frozen blackberries, drained, *divided*

Whipped cream

In a bowl, combine the flour, sugar and baking powder. Cut in butter until mixture resembles coarse crumbs. Stir in egg until dough forms a ball. Press onto the bottom and 2 in. up the sides of an ungreased 9-in. springform pan.

For filling, in a bowl, beat the egg yolks, sour cream, sugar and vanilla just until combined. Sprinkle 2 cups blackberries over crust. Carefully pour sour cream mixture over berries. Bake at 325° for 1-1/2 hours or until center is almost set. Cool on a wire rack (center will fall).

Remove sides of pan. Top with whipped cream and remaining blackberries. This dessert is best eaten the same day it's prepared. Refrigerate any leftovers. **Yield:** 12-14 servings.

Editor's Note: Even a tight-fitting springform pan may leak. To prevent drips, place the pan on a shallow baking pan in the oven.

Honey Baked Apples

These tender apples smell so good while they're in the oven—and taste even better. We enjoy the golden raisins inside and the soothing taste of honey. They're a yummy change from the cinnamon and sugar seasoning traditionally used with baked apples.
—Chere Bell
Colorado Springs, Colorado

2-1/4 cups water
  3/4 cup packed brown sugar
    3 tablespoons honey
    6 large tart apples
    1 cup golden raisins
Vanilla ice cream, optional

In a saucepan, bring water, brown sugar and honey to a boil. Remove from the heat.

Core the apples and peel the top third of each. Place apples in an ungreased 9-in. baking dish. Fill the apples with the raisins; sprinkle any remaining raisins into the pan. Pour the sugar syrup over the apples.

Bake, uncovered, at 350° for 1 hour or until the apples are tender, basting occasionally with the sugar syrup. Serve with ice cream if desired. **Yield:** 6 servings.

Strawberry Schaum Torte

(Pictured above)

This recipe was handed down from my German grandma. She took great pride in serving it.
—Diane Krisman, Hales Corners, Wisconsin

  8 egg whites (about 1 cup)
  2 cups sugar
  1 tablespoon white vinegar
  1 teaspoon vanilla extract
1/4 teaspoon salt
Sliced fresh strawberries
Whipped cream

In a large mixing bowl, beat the egg whites on high speed until soft peaks form. Reduce speed to medium. Add sugar, 2 tablespoons at a time, beating until stiff and glossy peaks form. Beat in the vinegar, vanilla and salt.

Spread into a greased 10-in. springform pan. Bake at 300° for 65-70 minutes or until lightly browned. Remove to a wire rack to cool (meringue will fall). Serve with strawberries and whipped cream. Store leftovers in the refrigerator. **Yield:** 10-12 servings.

Editor's Note: This recipe requires a stand mixer.

remaining dough covered with plastic wrap and a damp cloth. Brush one sheet with butter. Top with another sheet; brush with butter. Repeat with remaining phyllo and butter. Cut stack lengthwise into three pieces; cut widthwise into fourths. Lightly press each stack into a greased muffin cup.

In a blender, place the egg, lemon juice, vanilla, cheeses and sugar; cover and process until smooth. Spoon about 2 tablespoons into each phyllo cup. Bake at 350° for 12-15 minutes or until lightly browned. Carefully remove from pan to wire racks to cool. Cover and refrigerate.

For sauce, drain raspberries, reserving the juice in a small saucepan; set berries aside. Bring juice to a boil. Reduce heat; simmer, uncovered, for 15-20 minutes or until reduced to 3/4 cup. In a blender, puree reserved raspberries; press through a sieve to remove seeds. In a bowl, combine pureed raspberries, raspberry juice, sugar and lemon juice. Cover and refrigerate until chilled.

To serve, spoon raspberry sauce onto dessert plates; top each with a cheesecake cup. Garnish with fresh berries and mint. **Yield:** 12 servings.

Raspberry Cheesecake Cups

(Pictured above)

I'm frequently told these festive individual desserts are too pretty to eat! Phyllo dough is easy to work with—don't be afraid to try it for these special treats. With the bright red raspberries, these creamy cheese cups make a fine finale for Christmas dinner. —Brad Moritz
Limerick, Pennsylvania

    8 sheets phyllo dough
1/4 cup butter, melted
    1 egg
    1 teaspoon lemon juice
1/2 teaspoon vanilla extract
    1 package (8 ounces) cream cheese,
      cubed
1/2 cup small-curd cottage cheese
    3 tablespoons sugar
RASPBERRY SAUCE:
    3 packages (10 ounces *each*) frozen
      sweetened raspberries, thawed
1/4 cup sugar
    1 tablespoon lemon juice
Fresh raspberries and mint

Unroll phyllo dough sheets; trim if necessary into 13-in. x 9-in. rectangles. While assembling, keep

Strawberry Peach Melba

(Pictured on page 117)

I get oohs and aahs when setting out this cool, fruity dessert. It combines my three all-time favorites—peaches, strawberries and ice cream. It's so simple I can assemble it for company after we all finish the main course. —Marion Karlin
Waterloo, Iowa

    3 cups fresh *or* frozen whole strawberries
    1 cup confectioners' sugar
1/4 cup water
    1 teaspoon lemon juice
    2 teaspoons cornstarch
    1 tablespoon cold water
    1 teaspoon vanilla extract
    4 slices *or* scoops vanilla ice cream
    1 can (15 ounces) sliced peaches, drained
Whipped topping

In a saucepan, mash strawberries; add sugar, water and lemon juice. Cook and stir until mixture comes to a boil. Combine the cornstarch and cold water until smooth; stir into the strawberry mixture. Cook and stir for 2 minutes or until thickened and bubbly.

Remove from the heat; stir in vanilla. Strain to remove the pulp. Place the pan in an ice-water bath to cool, stirring occasionally. Serve strawberry sauce over ice cream; top with peaches and whipped topping. **Yield:** 4 servings.

Plum Kuchen

I remember my mother making plum kuchen. She never followed a recipe, but this recipe tastes just like hers. —Gretchen Berendt
Carroll Valley, Pennsylvania

2 eggs
1/3 cup milk
3 tablespoons butter, melted
1 cup all-purpose flour
1/2 cup plus 2 tablespoons sugar,
 divided
1 teaspoon baking powder
1-1/4 teaspoons ground cinnamon,
 divided
1/4 teaspoon salt
1/4 teaspoon ground nutmeg
6 medium plums, pitted and halved
Whipped cream and additional ground
 nutmeg, optional

In a mixing bowl, beat the eggs, milk and butter. Combine the flour, 1/2 cup sugar, baking powder, 3/4 teaspoon cinnamon, salt and nutmeg; add to the egg mixture and beat just until combined. Pour into a greased 9-in. round baking pan. Place plums cut side up over batter. Combine remaining sugar and cinnamon; sprinkle over the top.

Bake at 375° for 20-25 minutes or until a toothpick inserted near the center comes out clean. Cool for 10 minutes before removing from pan to a wire rack to cool completely. Serve kuchen with whipped cream and sprinkle with nutmeg if desired. **Yield:** 6 servings.

Easy Rhubarb Dessert

This is a very tasty and attractive dessert, yet it's simple to prepare. It's great served warm with ice cream. —Mildred Mesick, Richmond, New York

4 cups sliced fresh *or* frozen rhubarb
1 package (3 ounces) raspberry gelatin
1/3 cup sugar
1 package (18-1/4 ounces) yellow *or* white
 cake mix
1 cup water
1/3 cup butter, melted
Ice cream, optional

Place rhubarb in a greased 13-in. x 9-in. x 2-in. baking dish. Sprinkle with the gelatin, sugar and cake mix. Pour water evenly over dry ingredients; drizzle with butter. Bake at 350° for 1 hour or until rhubarb is tender. Serve with ice cream if desired. **Yield:** 16-20 servings.

Poached Pear Surprise

(Pictured below)

Pears are my husband's favorite fruit, so he immediately declared this dessert "a keeper." It's elegant but easy, satisfying yet light. —Barbara Smith
Cannon Falls, Minnesota

4 medium ripe pears
1 cup water
1/2 cup sugar
1 teaspoon vanilla extract
1/3 cup finely chopped walnuts
2 tablespoons confectioners' sugar
1 teaspoon milk
CHOCOLATE SAUCE:
1/3 cup water
1/3 cup sugar
1/4 cup butter
1-1/3 cups semisweet chocolate chips
Fresh mint, optional

Core pears from bottom, leaving stems intact. Peel pears. Cut 1/4 in. from bottom to level if necessary. In a saucepan, bring water and sugar to a boil. Add pears; reduce heat. Cover and simmer for 10-15 minutes or until tender. Remove from heat; stir vanilla into sugar syrup. Spoon over pears. Cover; refrigerate until chilled. Meanwhile, combine walnuts, confectioners' sugar and milk; set aside.

For chocolate sauce, combine water, sugar and butter in a small saucepan; bring to a boil. Remove from the heat; stir in chocolate chips until melted. To serve, drain pears well; spoon nut mixture into cavities. Place on dessert plates; top with some of the chocolate sauce. Insert a mint leaf near stem if desired. Serve with the remaining chocolate sauce. **Yield:** 4 servings.

Sensational Strawberry Shortcake

(Pictured below)

I love to pick strawberries in the morning, then make this shortcake in the afternoon. This pretty dessert really hits the spot on a hot summer day.
—Sarah Martin, Ridgeland, Mississippi

    1 quart strawberries, sliced
    1 cup sugar, *divided*
    2 cups all-purpose flour
    1 tablespoon plus 1 teaspoon baking
      powder
    1/4 teaspoon salt
Dash ground nutmeg
    1/2 cup butter
    1/2 cup milk
    2 eggs, *separated*
    2 to 3 cups sweetened whipped cream
Fresh mint, optional

In a bowl, gently stir strawberries and 1/2 cup sugar; chill. Meanwhile, in another bowl, combine flour, 1/4 cup sugar, baking powder, salt and nutmeg; cut in butter until crumbly. Combine milk and egg yolks; mix well. Add to crumb mixture, stirring just until moistened. Divide and pat into two greased 9-in. round cake pans.

In a small mixing bowl, beat egg whites until stiff peaks form; spread over dough. Sprinkle with remaining sugar. Bake at 300° for 40-45 minutes or until golden. Cool 10 minutes before removing from pan to a wire rack. (Layers will be thin.) Cool completely.

Place one cake layer on a large serving plate; spread with half of the whipped cream. Spoon half of the strawberries over cream. Repeat layers. Garnish with mint if desired. **Yield:** 8-10 servings.

Editor's Note: This dessert is best when served the same day as prepared.

Peanut Butter Berry Delights

These cream-filled, chocolate-dipped berries make a fun snack for a shower or a pretty party dessert that inspires compliments.
—Rose Harman
Hays, Kansas

    1/2 cup creamy peanut butter
    5 tablespoons milk chocolate chips,
      melted and cooled
    2 tablespoons whipped topping
    20 to 25 large fresh strawberries
    5 squares (1 ounce *each*) semisweet
      chocolate, melted

Line a baking sheet with waxed paper; set aside. In a small bowl, combine the peanut butter, melted milk chocolate and whipped topping.

Beginning at the right of the stem, cut each strawberry in half diagonally. Scoop out the white portion from the larger half of each berry. Spread or pipe peanut butter mixture between the two halves; press gently.

Place on prepared pan; refrigerate for 15 minutes or until set. Dip bottom half of berries in semisweet chocolate. Place on pan. Refrigerate for 15-20 minutes or until set. **Yield:** 20-25 servings.

Editor's Note: Reduced-fat or generic brands of peanut butter are not recommended for this recipe.

Pear Melba Dumplings

I substituted pears in a favorite apple dumpling recipe, then added a raspberry sauce for this delicious variation.
—Doreen Kelly
Roslyn, Pennsylvania

    2 cups all-purpose flour
1-1/4 teaspoons salt
    1/2 teaspoon cornstarch
    2/3 cup butter-flavored shortening
    4 to 5 tablespoons cold water
    6 small ripe pears, peeled and cored
    6 tablespoons brown sugar
    1/4 teaspoon ground cinnamon
    2 tablespoons milk
    1 tablespoon sugar

RASPBERRY SAUCE:
- 1 tablespoon sugar
- 1 tablespoon cornstarch
- 2 tablespoons water
- 1 package (10 ounces) frozen raspberries, thawed
- 1/4 teaspoon almond extract

Ice cream, optional

In a bowl, combine flour, salt and cornstarch. Cut in shortening until mixture resembles coarse crumbs. Stir in water until pastry forms a ball. On a floured surface, roll into a 21-in. x 14-in. rectangle. Cut into six squares.

Place one pear in center of each square. Pack pear centers with brown sugar; sprinkle with cinnamon. Brush edges of squares with milk; fold up corners to center and pinch to seal. Place in a greased 15-in. x 10-in. x 1-in. baking pan. Brush with milk; sprinkle with sugar. Bake at 375° for 35-40 minutes or until golden brown.

Meanwhile, in a saucepan, combine sugar, cornstarch and water until smooth. Add raspberries. Bring to a boil; cook and stir for 2 minutes or until thickened. Remove from the heat; stir in extract. Serve warm over warm dumplings with ice cream if desired. **Yield:** 6 servings.

Northern Cherry Puffs

Michigan is the top cherry-producing state in the country. This is one of my family's favorite cherry recipes. —Barbara Hanmer, Benzonia, Michigan

- 1 cup fresh *or* frozen pitted dark sweet cherries, thawed and drained
- 1 tablespoon lemon juice
- 1-1/2 teaspoons almond extract, *divided*
- 1/4 teaspoon red food coloring, optional
- 1/3 cup shortening
- 2/3 cup sugar
- 1 egg
- 1 cup all-purpose flour
- 1/2 teaspoon salt
- 1/2 teaspoon baking powder
- 1/3 cup milk

SAUCE:
- 1/2 cup sugar
- 4-1/2 teaspoons cornstarch
- 1/4 cup water
- 2 cups fresh *or* frozen pitted dark sweet cherries
- 1/4 teaspoon red food coloring, optional

Whipped cream *or* ice cream

In a bowl, combine cherries, lemon juice, 1/2 teaspoon extract and food coloring if desired; toss to coat. Spoon into four greased 10-oz. custard cups.

In a mixing bowl, cream shortening and sugar. Beat in egg and remaining extract. Combine flour, salt and baking powder; add to the creamed mixture alternately with milk. Spoon over cherry mixture. Bake at 375° for 20-25 minutes or until golden brown. Cool in cups for 10 minutes.

Meanwhile, in a saucepan, combine sugar and cornstarch. Stir in water, cherries and food coloring if desired until blended. Bring to a boil over medium heat; cook and stir for 2 minutes or until thickened. Invert puffs onto dessert plates; top with warm cherry sauce and whipped cream. **Yield:** 4 servings.

Raspberry Cream Croissants

(Pictured above)

A friend and I came up with this recipe. She likes it with strawberries, but I prefer raspberries.
—Sherry Horton, Sioux Falls, South Dakota

- 4 to 6 croissants
- 1/2 cup seedless raspberry jam
- Whipped cream in a can *or* whipped topping
- 1-1/4 cups fresh *or* frozen unsweetened raspberries, thawed
- Confectioners' sugar, optional

Cut the croissants in half horizontally; spread cut halves with jam. Spread whipped cream over bottom halves; top with raspberries. Replace tops. Dust with confectioners' sugar if desired. Serve immediately. **Yield:** 4-6 servings.

INDEX